TOMÁŠ MASARYK

TOMÁŠ MASARYK

Gavin Lewis

CHELSEA HOUSE PUBLISHERS
NEW YORK
PHILADELPHIA

Chelsea House Publishers
EDITOR-IN-CHIEF: Nancy Toff
EXECUTIVE EDITOR: Remmel T. Nunn
MANAGING EDITOR: Karyn Gullen Browne
COPY CHIEF: Juliann Barbato
PICTURE EDITOR: Adrian G. Allen
ART DIRECTOR: Maria Epes
MANUFACTURING MANAGER: Gerald Levine

World Leaders—Past & Present
SENIOR EDITOR: John W. Selfridge

Staff for TOMÁŠ MASARYK
COPY EDITOR: Mark Rifkin
DEPUTY COPY CHIEF: Nicole Bowen
EDITORIAL ASSISTANT: Nate Eaton
PICTURE RESEARCHER: Andrea Reithmayr
ASSISTANT ART DIRECTOR: Loraine Machlin
DESIGNER: David Murray
DESIGN ASSISTANT: James Baker
PRODUCTION MANAGER: Joseph Romano
PRODUCTION COORDINATOR: Marie Claire Cebrián
COVER ILLUSTRATION: Bill Donahey

First Printing

1 3 5 7 9 8 6 4 2

Library of Congress Cataloging in Publication Data

Lewis, Gavin.
   Tomáš Masaryk / Gavin Lewis.
   p.   cm.—(World leaders past & present)
   Bibliography: p.
   Includes index.
   Summary: A biography of the scholar and statesman who helped
found Czechoslovakia in 1918 and served as its first president from
1918 until 1935.
ISBN 1-55546-816-0
     0-7910-0699-9 (pbk.)
   1. Masaryk, T. G. (Tomáš Garrigue), 1850–1937—Juvenile
literature. 2. Presidents—Czechoslovakia—Biography—Juvenile
literature. [1. Masaryk, T. G. (Tomáš Garrigue), 1850–1937.
2. Presidents—Czechoslovakia.] I. Title. II. Series.
DB2191.M38L48   1989
943.7′032′092—dc20   89-33131
[B]   CIP
[92]   AC

Contents

John Adams
John Quincy Adams
Konrad Adenauer
Alexander the Great
Salvador Allende
Marc Antony
Corazon Aquino
Yasir Arafat
King Arthur
Hafez al-Assad
Kemal Atatürk
Attila
Clement Attlee
Augustus Caesar
Menachem Begin
David Ben-Gurion
Otto von Bismarck
Léon Blum
Simon Bolívar
Cesare Borgia
Willy Brandt
Leonid Brezhnev
Julius Caesar
John Calvin
Jimmy Carter
Fidel Castro
Catherine the Great
Charlemagne
Chiang Kai-Shek
Winston Churchill
Georges Clemenceau
Cleopatra
Constantine the Great
Hernán Cortés
Oliver Cromwell
Georges-Jacques
  Danton
Jefferson Davis
Moshe Dayan
Charles de Gaulle
Eamon De Valera
Eugene Debs
Deng Xiaoping
Benjamin Disraeli
Alexander Dubček
François & Jean-Claude
  Duvalier
Dwight Eisenhower
Eleanor of Aquitaine
Elizabeth I
Faisal
Ferdinand & Isabella
Francisco Franco
Benjamin Franklin

Frederick the Great
Indira Gandhi
Mohandas Gandhi
Giuseppe Garibaldi
Amin & Bashir Gemayel
Genghis Khan
William Gladstone
Mikhail Gorbachev
Ulysses S. Grant
Ernesto "Che" Guevara
Tenzin Gyatso
Alexander Hamilton
Dag Hammarskjöld
Henry VIII
Henry of Navarre
Paul von Hindenburg
Hirohito
Adolf Hitler
Ho Chi Minh
King Hussein
Ivan the Terrible
Andrew Jackson
James I
Wojciech Jaruzelski
Thomas Jefferson
Joan of Arc
Pope John XXIII
Pope John Paul II
Lyndon Johnson
Benito Juárez
John Kennedy
Robert Kennedy
Jomo Kenyatta
Ayatollah Khomeini
Nikita Khrushchev
Kim Il Sung
Martin Luther King, Jr.
Henry Kissinger
Kublai Khan
Lafayette
Robert E. Lee
Vladimir Lenin
Abraham Lincoln
David Lloyd George
Louis XIV
Martin Luther
Judas Maccabeus
James Madison
Nelson & Winnie
  Mandela
Mao Zedong
Ferdinand Marcos
George Marshall

Mary, Queen of Scots
Tomáš Masaryk
Golda Meir
Klemens von Metternich
James Monroe
Hosni Mubarak
Robert Mugabe
Benito Mussolini
Napoléon Bonaparte
Gamal Abdel Nasser
Jawaharlal Nehru
Nero
Nicholas II
Richard Nixon
Kwame Nkrumah
Daniel Ortega
Mohammed Reza Pahlavi
Thomas Paine
Charles Stewart
  Parnell
Pericles
Juan Perón
Peter the Great
Pol Pot
Muammar el-Qaddafi
Ronald Reagan
Cardinal Richelieu
Maximilien Robespierre
Eleanor Roosevelt
Franklin Roosevelt
Theodore Roosevelt
Anwar Sadat
Haile Selassie
Prince Sihanouk
Jan Smuts
Joseph Stalin
Sukarno
Sun Yat-sen
Tamerlane
Mother Teresa
Margaret Thatcher
Josip Broz Tito
Toussaint L'Ouverture
Leon Trotsky
Pierre Trudeau
Harry Truman
Queen Victoria
Lech Walesa
George Washington
Chaim Weizmann
Woodrow Wilson
Xerxes
Emiliano Zapata
Zhou Enlai

CHELSEA HOUSE PUBLISHERS

ON LEADERSHIP

Arthur M. Schlesinger, jr.

LEADERSHIP, it may be said, is really what makes the world go round. Love no doubt smooths the passage; but love is a private transaction between consenting adults. Leadership is a public transaction with history. The idea of leadership affirms the capacity of individuals to move, inspire, and mobilize masses of people so that they act together in pursuit of an end. Sometimes leadership serves good purposes, sometimes bad; but whether the end is benign or evil, great leaders are those men and women who leave their personal stamp on history.

Now, the very concept of leadership implies the proposition that individuals can make a difference. This proposition has never been universally accepted. From classical times to the present day, eminent thinkers have regarded individuals as no more than the agents and pawns of larger forces, whether the gods and goddesses of the ancient world or, in the modern era, race, class, nation, the dialectic, the will of the people, the spirit of the times, history itself. Against such forces, the individual dwindles into insignificance.

So contends the thesis of historical determinism. Tolstoy's great novel *War and Peace* offers a famous statement of the case. Why, Tolstoy asked, did millions of men in the Napoleonic Wars, denying their human feelings and their common sense, move back and forth across Europe slaughtering their fellows? "The war," Tolstoy answered, "was bound to happen simply because it was bound to happen." All prior history predetermined it. As for leaders, they, Tolstoy said, "are but the labels that serve to give a name to an end and, like labels, they have the least possible connection with the event." The greater the leader, "the more conspicuous the inevitability and the predestination of every act he commits." The leader, said Tolstoy, is "the slave of history."

Determinism takes many forms. Marxism is the determinism of class. Nazism the determinism of race. But the idea of men and women as the slaves of history runs athwart the deepest human instincts. Rigid determinism abolishes the idea of human freedom—

the assumption of free choice that underlies every move we make, every word we speak, every thought we think. It abolishes the idea of human responsibility, since it is manifestly unfair to reward or punish people for actions that are by definition beyond their control. No one can live consistently by any deterministic creed. The Marxist states prove this themselves by their extreme susceptibility to the cult of leadership.

More than that, history refutes the idea that individuals make no difference. In December 1931 a British politician crossing Park Avenue in New York City between 76th and 77th Streets around 10:30 P.M. looked in the wrong direction and was knocked down by an automobile—a moment, he later recalled, of a man aghast, a world aglare: "I do not understand why I was not broken like an eggshell or squashed like a gooseberry." Fourteen months later an American politician, sitting in an open car in Miami, Florida, was fired on by an assassin; the man beside him was hit. Those who believe that individuals make no difference to history might well ponder whether the next two decades would have been the same had Mario Constasino's car killed Winston Churchill in 1931 and Giuseppe Zangara's bullet killed Franklin Roosevelt in 1933. Suppose, in addition, that Adolf Hitler had been killed in the street fighting during the Munich *Putsch* of 1923 and that Lenin had died of typhus during World War I. What would the 20th century be like now?

For better or for worse, individuals do make a difference. "The notion that a people can run itself and its affairs anonymously," wrote the philosopher William James, "is now well known to be the silliest of absurdities. Mankind does nothing save through initiatives on the part of inventors, great or small, and imitation by the rest of us—these are the sole factors in human progress. Individuals of genius show the way, and set the patterns, which common people then adopt and follow."

Leadership, James suggests, means leadership in thought as well as in action. In the long run, leaders in thought may well make the greater difference to the world. But, as Woodrow Wilson once said, "Those only are leaders of men, in the general eye, who lead in action. . . . It is at their hands that new thought gets its trans-lation into the crude language of deeds." Leaders in thought often invent in solitude and obscurity, leaving to later generations the tasks of imitation. Leaders in action—the leaders portrayed in this series—have to be effective in their own time.

And they cannot be effective by themselves. They must act in response to the rhythms of their age. Their genius must be adapted, in a phrase of William James's, "to the receptivities of the moment." Leaders are useless without followers. "There goes the mob," said the French politician hearing a clamor in the streets. "I am their leader. I must follow them." Great leaders turn the inchoate emotions of the mob to purposes of their own. They seize on the opportunities of their time, the hopes, fears, frustrations, crises, potentialities. They succeed when events have prepared the way for them, when the community is awaiting to be aroused, when they can provide the clarifying and organizing ideas. Leadership ignites the circuit between the individual and the mass and thereby alters history.

It may alter history for better or for worse. Leaders have been responsible for the most extravagant follies and most monstrous crimes that have beset suffering humanity. They have also been vital in such gains as humanity has made in individual freedom, religious and racial tolerance, social justice, and respect for human rights.

There is no sure way to tell in advance who is going to lead for good and who for evil. But a glance at the gallery of men and women in *World Leaders—Past and Present* suggests some useful tests.

One test is this: Do leaders lead by force or by persuasion? By command or by consent? Through most of history leadership was exercised by the divine right of authority. The duty of followers was to defer and to obey. "Theirs not to reason why / Theirs but to do and die." On occasion, as with the so-called enlightened despots of the 18th century in Europe, absolutist leadership was animated by humane purposes. More often, absolutism nourished the passion for domination, land, gold, and conquest and resulted in tyranny.

The great revolution of modern times has been the revolution of equality. The idea that all people should be equal in their legal condition has undermined the old structure of authority, hierarchy, and deference. The revolution of equality has had two contrary effects on the nature of leadership. For equality, as Alexis de Tocqueville pointed out in his great study *Democracy in America*, might mean equality in servitude as well as equality in freedom.

"I know of only two methods of establishing equality in the political world," Tocqueville wrote. "Rights must be given to every citizen, or none at all to anyone . . . save one, who is the master of all." There was no middle ground "between the sovereignty of all and the absolute power of one man." In his astonishing prediction of 20th-century totalitarian dictatorship, Tocqueville explained how the revolution of equality could lead to the *"Führerprinzip"* and more terrible absolutism than the world had ever known.

But when rights are given to every citizen and the sovereignty of all is established, the problem of leadership takes a new form, becomes more exacting than ever before. It is easy to issue commands and enforce them by the rope and the stake, the concentration camp and the *gulag.* It is much harder to use argument and achievement to overcome opposition and win consent. The Founding Fathers of the United States understood the difficulty. They believed that history had given them the opportunity to decide, as Alexander Hamilton wrote in the first Federalist Paper, whether men are indeed capable of basing government on "reflection and choice, or whether they are forever destined to depend . . . on accident and force."

Government by reflection and choice called for a new style of leadership and a new quality of followership. It required leaders to be responsive to popular concerns, and it required followers to be active and informed participants in the process. Democracy does not eliminate emotion from politics; sometimes it fosters demagoguery; but it is confident that, as the greatest of democratic leaders put it, you cannot fool all of the people all of the time. It measures leadership by results and retires those who overreach or falter or fail.

It is true that in the long run despots are measured by results too. But they can postpone the day of judgment, sometimes indefinitely, and in the meantime they can do infinite harm. It is also true that democracy is no guarantee of virtue and intelligence in government, for the voice of the people is not necessarily the voice of God. But democracy, by assuring the right of opposition, offers built-in resistance to the evils inherent in absolutism. As the theologian Reinhold Niebuhr summed it up, "Man's capacity for justice makes democracy possible, but man's inclination to injustice makes democracy necessary."

A second test for leadership is the end for which power is sought. When leaders have as their goal the supremacy of a master race or the promotion of totalitarian revolution or the acquisition and exploitation of colonies or the protection of greed and privilege or the preservation of personal power, it is likely that their leadership will do little to advance the cause of humanity. When their goal is the abolition of slavery, the liberation of women, the enlargement of opportunity for the poor and powerless, the extension of equal rights to racial minorities, the defense of the freedoms of expression and opposition, it is likely that their leadership will increase the sum of human liberty and welfare.

Leaders have done great harm to the world. They have also conferred great benefits. You will find both sorts in this series. Even "good" leaders must be regarded with a certain wariness. Leaders are not demigods; they put on their trousers one leg after another just like ordinary mortals. No leader is infallible, and every leader needs to be reminded of this at regular intervals. Irreverence irritates leaders but is their salvation. Unquestioning submission corrupts leaders and demeans followers. Making a cult of a leader is always a mistake. Fortunately hero worship generates its own antidote. "Every hero," said Emerson, "becomes a bore at last."

The signal benefit the great leaders confer is to embolden the rest of us to live according to our own best selves, to be active, insistent, and resolute in affirming our own sense of things. For great leaders attest to the reality of human freedom against the supposed inevitabilities of history. And they attest to the wisdom and power that may lie within the most unlikely of us, which is why Abraham Lincoln remains the supreme example of great leadership. A great leader, said Emerson, exhibits new possibilities to all humanity. "We feed on genius. . . . Great men exist that there may be greater men."

Great leaders, in short, justify themselves by emancipating and empowering their followers. So humanity struggles to master its destiny, remembering with Alexis de Tocqueville: "It is true that around every man a fatal circle is traced beyond which he cannot pass; but within the wide verge of that circle he is powerful and free; as it is with man, so with communities."

1

The Homecoming

It was December 21, 1918. Six weeks earlier, World War I had come to an end. In the central European city of Prague — "hundred-towered Prague," as its proud citizens called it — church spires and the roofs of palaces stood out against the blue sky of a mild winter's day. A couple of months earlier, Prague had been a provincial city in the empire of Austria-Hungary, which along with Germany and Turkey, had been on the losing side in the Great War. But instead of mourning the empire's defeat, the city was celebrating a joyful public holiday.

The schools were closed, the factories lay idle, every store and office was locked and shuttered, and even the streetcars had stopped running for the day. In the center of the city, excited crowds totaling half a million people had assembled. Factory workers, upper-class citizens, discharged soldiers, schoolchildren, and peasants from the nearby countryside thronged the streets. Every building was decorated with flags. There were the flags of France, Britain, Italy, and the United States, the countries that had defeated Austria-Hungary and its allies. Everywhere, too, there flew the flag of a new independent republic, Czechoslovakia, just eight weeks old, of which Prague was now the capital city.

> *If you love your country do not talk about it, but do something worthwhile; that is all that matters.*
> —TOMÁŠ MASARYK

Virtually all his life, Tomáš Masaryk dreamed of the day when Czechs and Slovaks would unite to form a single Czechoslovak state, free from the stifling rule of the Hapsburgs. In 1918, the dream came true mainly as a result of Masaryk's own courage and dedication.

For the people of Prague, the defeat of Austria-Hungary was in fact a victory. They were Czechs, members of a proud and once independent nation that for four centuries had been subject to the ruling dynasty of Austria-Hungary, the Hapsburgs. The defeat of their rulers had enabled the Czechs at long last to regain their independence. They had joined together with a neighboring nation very similar in language and ethnic origins and also long subject to Hapsburg rule, the Slovaks. Together, the two nations would enjoy freedom and democracy in the Czechoslovak republic.

That was not the only reason the people of Prague were celebrating. On this particular day, they were to welcome home the leader and liberator of the Czechs and Slovaks. He had spent the war years as an exile and "traitor," working for the cause of Czechoslovak independence. Now he was coming home as the new republic's first president. His name was Tomáš Garrigue Masaryk.

An artist's depiction of Masaryk's triumphant return to Prague in December 1918. Throughout its history, Prague has been a proud and beautiful city, but for more than 200 years its growth and prosperity have been hindered by imperial powers.

Shortly after one o'clock, as cannons thundered in salute from the hills above the city's towers, the train bringing the "president-liberator" back from exile pulled into Prague's main railroad station. An army band struck up the Czech, and then the Slovak, national anthem. A tall, lean, bearded man stepped out of the presidential car and stood once more on the streets of the city that he had left four years before, not knowing if he would ever set foot on them again. While the band played the anthems of the countries that had won the war and helped Czechoslovakia to freedom, Masaryk stood at attention, his face strong and determined. With his balding head, his white beard and mustache, and his thoughtful gray eyes behind old-fashioned pince-nez spectacles, Masaryk looked more like an elderly professor than the liberator of two nations. Yet at the sight of him the Czechoslovak political leaders who had spent the war years at home wept for joy.

Masaryk himself could hardly speak for emotion. His first public words, in reply to a speech of welcome from a leading politician, were "Excuse me if I don't say much. To tell the truth, I don't know what I should say to you." There was a long pause while he fought back his tears. Finally he managed to say, "In four years, this is the first time that I've been so moved. . . . I know, and you all know, that we have a great deal of work ahead of us. . . . I know Austria-Hungary, and I know how they pressured you, but you weren't intimidated, you stuck it out and you stayed strong. . . . I promise you that just as I've worked up to now and done my best to stay healthy, I'll go on working with you in the future as well."

The speech was typical of Masaryk, as a man and as a leader: Though he was returning as his nation's greatest hero, he made a speech completely without heroics. Instead, what he mainly talked about was work: The work that he and others had done to make Czechoslovakia independent, and the work that would have to be done in the future to make it strong.

Outside the railroad station, it was the turn of the ordinary people of Prague to welcome their lib-

> *It is a great thing when a small country among great ones does not get left behind but takes its share in the work of bettering humanity.*
> —TOMÁŠ MASARYK

The people of Prague welcome the revered liberator of the Czechs and Slovaks, Tomáš Garrigue Masaryk, back to his homeland in December 1918. Masaryk, who had spent the World War I years in exile in western Europe, was sworn in as president of the newly formed Republic of Czechoslovakia on the day of his return.

erator. For hours, Masaryk's car moved through the city, making its way along a narrow path through the jubilant masses in the streets. Masaryk's daughters rode behind his car in what had been the imperial state coach, drawn by two white horses. Masaryk had refused to ride in it himself, so the citizens of Prague would have to be satisfied with seeing their liberator's family in the coach that had once carried the Hapsburg rulers.

Masaryk's route was carefully chosen to take him past Prague's many monuments of the glorious and tragic history of the Czech nation. He drove down Wenceslas Square, named after a great Czech king and saint of the Middle Ages, the "good king Wenceslas" of the Christmas carol. The huge square, nearly half a mile long, was jammed with people who cheered and sang the Czech and Slovak national anthems as Masaryk passed. They shouted, "Welcome home, Daddy Masaryk!" (Czech and Slovak soldiers fighting against Austria-Hungary had given Masaryk the nickname during the war.) He passed by the National Theater, a magnificent building constructed with the contributions of thousands of ordinary Czechs during the National Awakening, a 19th-century revival of Czech civilization. From the

theater balcony, trumpeters greeted the president with fanfares from an opera by Czech composer Bedřich Smetana. The procession then paused in the Old Town Square, where nearly three centuries earlier, in 1621, seven leaders of an unsuccessful rebellion against the Hapsburgs had been beheaded. Now, Masaryk, the leader of a successful revolution against the Hapsburgs, was welcomed in the square by the mayor of Prague.

Finally, in the evening, the festivities ended with a reception in Prague Castle, originally a fortress and later a magnificent palace, whose towers dominate the city's skyline. After the reception, President Masaryk retired for the night in a private apartment in the castle. From now on, the thousand-year-old residence of kings and emperors would be his home.

It was a remarkable destiny for a man who had been born 68 years earlier as the son of a coachman on an estate belonging to the Hapsburg emperors. What follows is the story of how this man of humble origin, who spent most of his career as a scholar and a maverick politician, was able in his old age to help overthrow an empire, found a republic, and liberate two nations.

2

The Young Rebel

Masaryk's road to the Prague Castle began 150 miles to the east, in the small town of Hodonín in the province of Moravia, where he was born on March 7, 1850. His family moved many times during his boyhood, as his father's work took him to different farms and estates. But always they stayed within the same county-sized district of villages and small towns connected by roads lined with fruit trees, where fields of wheat and rye, vineyards and forests stretched for many miles across the flat countryside.

Here Masaryk spent a typical country boyhood, playing the same kinds of tricks and getting into the same kinds of trouble that would have been perfectly familiar to Tom Sawyer or Huckleberry Finn. Toward the end of his life, he told the Czech writer Karel Čapek:

> A boy brought up in the country has a lot to learn! I should say so! He must know how to whistle with his lips, between his teeth, with one finger, with two, with his fist; then how to snap his fingers in two different ways; he must know all sorts of fighting, how to stand on his head, walk on his hands, and turn cartwheels; and above all how to run, that's the main thing.

Coming from an ethnically mixed area [Masaryk] was a conscientious student of languages, which were to enable him to read the treasures of foreign literature in the original.
—HANUS J. HAJEK
Masaryk biographer

Masaryk at the age of 13. Though studious and introspective as a boy, Tomáš had a rebellious streak that often got him into trouble with priests and school administrators.

In some ways, however, Masaryk's life was very different from that of an American boy of that time. He was growing up in a country, Austria-Hungary, where there lived not just one nation speaking one language, but many different nations speaking different languages, and all living under the rule of the Hapsburg emperor.

Even in Tomáš's own family, several different languages were spoken. With his playmates he spoke a local dialect, a mixture of the Czech and Slovak languages, because the district where he lived was on the border between the territories of the Czechs and the Slovaks. But he said his prayers in German, because he had been taught them by his mother, who had spent much of her life in a nearby German-speaking town and spoke that language better than Czech. Tomáš's father, on the other hand, came from a village a few miles farther east, in the territory of the Slovaks, and spoke to his son in Slovak. Was Tomáš a Czech, a German, or a Slovak? As a youngster, learning to turn cartwheels and whistle through his teeth, he neither knew nor cared.

But there was something else about his life that Tomáš knew about only too well and which he deeply

As a boy, Masaryk lived with his parents in this small house in the countryside east of Prague. The Masaryk family moved several times during Tomáš's childhood but never far from the town of Hodonín, where Tomáš was born in 1850.

hated. He was growing up in a world where some were highborn and others were humbler, where some were entitled to command and others had only the duty to obey. One day a party of noblemen came visiting to spend the day hunting in a local forest. After their day's sport, they were served a meal in the big house on the estate, and then the leftovers were distributed to the local peasants. Tomáš saw grown men and women fighting like animals for the scraps of the noblemen's elegant dinner. He ran away and wept—not with shame or pity but with fury. How could the nobles humiliate the peasants in this way? How could the peasants cooperate in their own humiliation? There was something in Tomáš that could not accept that this was right.

Tomáš, however, unlike most of his playmates, had a chance to rise out of the ranks of those who obeyed. He was one of the tiny minority of students bright enough to go on from the village school to high school. For Tomáš and his parents, this was a big risk: He would have to leave home, for high schools were few and far between, and he would miss the chance to learn a trade, such as coach driving or blacksmithing. Still, his mother wanted him to get an education, and in Tomáš's family, it was she who made the decisions. As Masaryk told Karel Čapek many years later, "It was my mother who had me sent to school, so that, as she said, I would not have to drudge like my parents."

As it turned out, the gamble paid off. As a student, and indeed throughout his life, Masaryk was an enthusiastic reader and learner. Even so, his school career was not an easy one. In high school, just as in the village, students were expected to be obedient to authority and to disguise or suppress whatever rebellious feelings or unorthodox ideas they might have. Tomáš was not good at that. What made his problems far worse was that in high school, he first encountered one of the basic features of life in Austria-Hungary: Among the many peoples under the Hapsburg emperors' rule, a few — among them the Germans — were privileged, while others, including the Czechs and Slovaks, were not.

Tomáš's father, Josef Masaryk, was a coachman on estates belonging to the Hapsburg emperors. A hardworking man and a lover of nature, Masaryk communicated these values to his son.

Tomáš Masaryk's mother, Tereza, made sure that her son received a formal education. Even though going off to school meant that he would miss the opportunity to learn a trade, Tomáš attended high school according to his mother's wishes.

In Tomáš's high school, located 60 miles from home in the city of Brno, the principal and most of the teachers and students were German, as was the language used in the classroom. There was nothing unusual about this; in fact it was the normal practice throughout the Czech territories. Czechs who wanted to get anything above a grade-school education had no choice but to learn German. After years of speaking, reading, and writing German in school and being reprimanded by their teachers and teased by their schoolmates for speaking Czech, they would often end by passing themselves off as Germans.

For Tomáš, with his mixed background, it would have been easy to "Germanize" himself in this way. But Tomáš, who had learned to loathe the unjust dictates of authority back in the village, was not about to humiliate himself by becoming a German simply because his teachers insisted that he do so. Instead, he joined the minority of students who identified themselves as Czechs and soon became known as one of the most unruly among them. He would be sent to the principal for such offenses as refusing to pronounce the Latin language with the "correct" German-style pronunciation or behaving rudely toward a teacher who was known to be a Germanized Czech.

Tomáš's rebellious nature got him into further trouble and almost ended his high school career when he began to doubt the truth of the Catholic faith in which he had been brought up. His doubts began as he observed the way his fellow students practiced their religion. Having just confessed their sins to the priest, not only would they be out committing the same sinful acts for which they had just asked forgiveness, but they would actually boast of it. To Tomáš, this seemed to show that the Catholic practice of confession was just a meaningless ritual that did not make people better but actually made them worse by adding hypocrisy to their other sins. Always one to act on his convictions, Tomáš then caused a scandal in the school by refusing to go to confession.

This was a very serious matter. Going to confession, like speaking and writing in German, was something that high school students were expected to do, whether they wanted to or not. Again Tomáš was sent to the principal, who told him that he did not believe in confession either, but, he declared, "I am an official, and I do what is expected of me." Tomáš replied, "Whoever acts against his own convictions is a scoundrel!" The furious principal started toward Tomáš, intending to throw him out of his office, and Tomáš picked up a poker from the fireplace to defend himself. The principal did not appreciate being called a scoundrel and being threatened with a poker by one of his own students. Shortly afterward, Tomáš received what was politely called "advice to depart."

The quarrel with the principal could have ended Tomáš's chances of getting an education, but it was followed by a stroke of luck. In order to pay for his food and lodging, Tomáš had been giving private lessons to wealthier but less talented students. One of these was the son of a very important man in Brno, the chief of police. In spite of being a police official and a German, this man respected and liked his son's uncompromising and forthright young teacher.

In 1872, Masaryk entered the University of Vienna, Austria-Hungary's leading institution of learning. There he studied philosophy, became involved in a Czech patriotic group, and contributed articles to *Osvěta*, a Czech monthly review.

Masaryk (seated, far left) with friends and colleagues in Leipzig in 1877. Awarded a doctoral degree from the University of Vienna, Masaryk then went to Leipzig for postgraduate study.

Just at this time, the chief of police gained a promotion: He was to do the same job but in Vienna, the imperial capital of Austria-Hungary. He took Tomáš with him and helped with his living expenses while the young man finished his high school education at one of the best schools in the city, where the students were mostly the sons of noblemen or of high-ranking officials of the emperor. From there, Tomáš gained admission to the University of Vienna, the leading university in Austria-Hungary. In spite of his proud and rebellious character and his insistence on being a Czech, he was on his way to joining the elite of the empire.

Masaryk was at the university from 1870 to 1882, first as a student and then as an unpaid lecturer. Here, at one of the greatest centers of learning in

Europe, he came into contact with ideas and knowledge from a field far wider than he had ever experienced before. Above all, in Vienna he first began to learn about something that was to influence his beliefs and actions for the rest of his life — the history, culture, and ways of thinking of the English-speaking countries, the United States and Britain. The methods of British philosophers, who stressed the value of reasoning from observed facts to proven conclusions, made a great impression on him, as his belief in the faith and miracles of the Catholic church grew ever weaker. The ideals of freedom and democracy, as embodied in the American republic, seemed to Masaryk to constitute a far nobler way of life than the world of unquestioned authority and unquestioning obedience that he had hated from his childhood.

Under the influence of these ideas, Masaryk reached a decision about his future: He would be a philosopher, a searcher for the truth about the world and the right way for people to live. This meant that in order to earn his living he would have to continue his university studies so as to qualify for a university teaching job. In 1876, therefore, he temporarily left Vienna to spend a year in Leipzig, Germany, where the university was noted for its training in philosophy. In Leipzig, Masaryk studied hard and learned a great deal. Also in Leipzig, something happened that Masaryk himself always regarded as even more important than his studies there: He fell in love.

It was an idealistic and serious-minded romance. The woman he courted, Charlotte Garrigue, was from Brooklyn, New York, and she was in Leipzig as part of a year-long tour of Europe. Masaryk was attracted to her because she was from a distant country that he admired, because she was self-confident, independent, highly intelligent, and above all, as he later told Čapek, because "she was absolutely uncompromising and utterly truthful." Together, they studied books on the major social and moral issues of the time. Among these was *On the Subjection of Women*, by the British thinker John Stuart Mill, one of the first writers to call for com-

While in Leipzig, Masaryk met Charlotte Garrigue, a young American woman who was studying and traveling in Europe for a year. Masaryk and "Charlie," as he called her, fell in love and were married in Brooklyn, New York, in 1878.

plete equality between women and men. By the time they left Leipzig—Masaryk to resume his studies in Vienna and "Charlie" to return home—they were engaged.

In 1878, Masaryk crossed the Atlantic and married Charlotte at Brooklyn City Hall. True to the belief in the equality of the sexes that Masaryk and his wife shared, he took her name. From that moment on, he was Tomáš Garrigue Masaryk.

At first, the newlyweds lived in a one-room apartment in Vienna. Masaryk's career had progressed so that he was now entitled to give unpaid lectures at the university while he worked on a thesis that would qualify him to apply for paid jobs. Even when his thesis was finished it was a hard struggle to find a job. There were not many professorships of philosophy, and they did not usually go to self-pro-

Masaryk returned to Vienna with his new bride and submitted a scholarly paper, *Suicide as a Collective Social Phenomenon in Modern Civilization*, to the faculty at the University of Vienna. The work, the cover of which is shown here, earned him an unpaid lectureship at the university.

DER SELBSTMORD

ALS

SOCIALE MASSENERSCHEINUNG

DER

MODERNEN CIVILISATION.

VON

Dᴿ THOMAS GARRIGUE MASARYK

DOCENT DER PHILOSOPHIE AN DER UNIVERSITÄT WIEN.

Greift nur hinein in's volle Menschenleben!
— wo ihr's packt, da ist's interessant.
Goethe.

WIEN, 1881.

VERLAG VON CARL KONEGEN.

claimed Czechs who believed in such things as democracy and equality of the sexes. For several years, Masaryk had to support his wife and a growing family — two sons and two daughters — by his old method of giving private lessons. Sometimes the income from wealthy students would not pay the bills, and at least once Masaryk had to humble himself by asking one of his professors for a loan.

Suddenly, Masaryk's luck changed. A new university was to be founded in Prague. There already was a university there, but it was dominated by Germans. In the new one, the professors and students were to be Czechs, teaching and studying in their own language. All of a sudden, Czechs with university-teaching qualifications were in demand. In 1882, at the age of 32, Masaryk became a professor at the Czech University of Prague.

It seemed that Masaryk was now set up for life. He had risen from humble beginnings to become a university professor, which in Austria-Hungary put him in the elite of society. He was happily married to a woman who shared his interests and ideals. Living and teaching among the people he had chosen to belong to, he could enjoy the peaceful and secure routine of a university professor for the rest of his life.

However, Masaryk, who, as a boy, had raged at the peasants for fighting over the noblemen's leftovers and had brandished a poker in the face of his high school principal, was not made for peace and security. The struggles and conflicts of his early life were over. Now the struggles and conflicts of his adult life would begin.

The Cathedral of St. Vitus, within the walls of the castle of Prague, dominates the city skyline. Masaryk returned to Prague in 1882, when he accepted a post as associate professor of philosophy at the newly founded Czech University there.

3

The Embattled Professor

Masaryk came to Prague at a time of both hope and frustration for the Czechs. Throughout Europe, this was a time of rising nationalism. Every nation was intent on developing its culture, its wealth, and its power. This included the Czechs, who were going through an era of progress that they themselves called the National Awakening. But Hapsburg power and German privilege still put barriers in the path of the Czechs, and no one knew how to break down these barriers.

For the Czechs, the National Awakening was actually a national revival. Long before, in the Middle Ages, they had been one of the foremost European nations. The three provinces in which they lived — Bohemia, Moravia, and Silesia — had together formed an independent kingdom that was one of the most prosperous and advanced of the time. Under the leadership of warlike religious dissidents, the Hussites, the Czech kingdom was powerful enough to defy the Catholic church and Catholic armies, and the Czechs eventually became a largely Protestant nation.

> *People seem not to understand that criticism, especially bitter criticism, is often a sign of self-criticism, a painful confession.*
> —TOMÁŠ MASARYK

Though Masaryk had become a university professor before the age of 30, he was not content simply to teach and write books: There was a Czech nationalist movement gaining momentum in his homeland, and he wanted to become part of it.

Czech theologian Jan Hus was burned at the stake in 1415 for propagating his unorthodox religious views. His followers, the Hussites, defied the Catholic church, forced numerous ecclesiastical reforms, and made the Czech kingdom into one of the foremost military powers in Europe.

Then, in 1526, the Czechs came under the rule of the Hapsburgs, a powerful dynasty of German origin and predominantly Catholic. The Hapsburgs also ruled many other nations and territories, and they were determined to make the Czechs obedient subjects of their empire. This led to Czech resistance and rebellions. After long struggles, these were finally crushed. Especially after the beheading of the rebels in 1621, the Czechs became little more than a nation of peasants. They worked as serfs, performing unpaid compulsory labor on the lands of German-speaking nobles. They paid their taxes to German-speaking officials of the emperor, whose offices were located in towns where all the burghers were Germans. They were forced to be Catholics, worshiping in churches with local Czech clergy but only under the supervision of German-speaking bishops.

From about 1750 on, however, the rule of the Hapsburgs became gradually less repressive. Some of the emperors genuinely wanted reforms, and others were forced by fear of revolution or defeat in war to make changes that would pacify their subjects. Protestant worship, long forbidden, was once again permitted. Serfdom was abolished. The Czech language, long despised as a mere dialect of illiterate villagers, began once again to be used in literature, science, and scholarship. Industrial development made Bohemia, Moravia, and Silesia the manufacturing heartland of Austria-Hungary. The sons and daughters of Czech peasants flocked to the towns to become factory workers, and often factory managers and owners as well, and the German burghers found themselves outnumbered. By the time that Masaryk was growing up, the National Awakening was in full swing, and the Czechs were on their way to regaining their old prominence among the European nations.

All the same, there was much that the Czechs still lacked. They were only 6 million strong, and they shared their 3 provinces with 3 million still-privileged Germans. Furthermore, there were 9 million Germans throughout Austria-Hungary and another 65 million in Germany itself. Moreover, the Czechs

Another religious reformer, Martin Luther, attacked the Roman Catholic church during the 16th-century religious movement known as the Reformation. As a result of the Reformation and the ascendancy of the Hussites, most Czechs left the Catholic church to become Protestants.

Hapsburg emperor Josef II operates a plow to experience firsthand the life of the Czech peasantry. The Hapsburgs, who took control of the Czech kingdom in 1526, ruled with an iron fist — prohibiting Protestant worship and subjecting the Czechs to rule by German-speaking nobles and officials — until around 1750, when they became less repressive.

were still ruled from a foreign city, Vienna, by a foreign dynasty, the Hapsburgs, whose goodwill they had reason to distrust. How could the Czechs continue to progress socially, politically, and culturally in the face of German privilege and Hapsburg power?

Among those who believed that they had answers to this question was Tomáš Masaryk. Although he was a professor of philosophy, Masaryk did not intend to be a head-in-the-clouds thinker. Instead, he lectured and wrote on social and moral problems, on religion and education, on science and scholarship. He was familiar with the progress and achievements of many nations in these fields — the British, the Americans, and also the much-resented Germans. It was by the standards of these and other nations that he judged the Czechs. Often it seemed to him that in spite of the National Awakening, they still lagged behind. Being a forthright and truthful man, he made it his business to say so. He began publishing a scholarly journal to expose the Czechs to the cultural achievements of other nations and to assess the Czechs' own intellectual, artistic, and scientific achievements. The assessments were mostly critical.

As a result, Masaryk soon became widely disliked. Senior professors at the university considered him a troublemaker, and most of the students, who tended to be ardently nationalistic, resented him. Rumors spread about him, based on his mixed background, his Viennese education, and his foreign wife: It was said that Masaryk was really a German or even an American, or at any rate, no real Czech.

Criticism of Masaryk turned to real hatred when he became embroiled in a scholarly dispute that turned into a major national scandal. The dispute concerned two collections of ancient manuscripts supposedly discovered by a pioneer of the National Awakening, Václav Hanka, in 1817 and 1818. The manuscripts contained poems, songs, and tales in the Czech language, some of which seemed to be nearly 1,000 years old. The Czechs were enormously proud of these manuscripts. A repressed and subjected people for three centuries, the Czechs did not have many things about which to be patriotic: They were not numerous or powerful; they had no system of government or way of life that was admired by other nations; in recent centuries, they had had no military victories about which they could boast. All they had was their glorious past and their cultural achievements. The manuscripts showed that the Czechs had a long cultural history comparable to those of the greatest European nations. The French and the English, the Russians and the Germans, all had their age-old literary masterpieces; so, it seemed, did the Czechs. The manuscripts, reverently preserved in the Bohemian Museum in Prague, were a national treasure to the Czechs.

There was only one problem: Quite a few distinguished scholars had reason to believe that the manuscripts were forged. The Czech language of the poems and tales and the handwriting they were in were not quite the same as those found in other documents of the time from which the manuscripts supposedly dated. But this was not just a scholarly question; it was one of Czech national pride. Anyone who voiced doubts about the manuscripts was liable to be accused of being unpatriotic, and so not many people did.

> *Go to the devil, loathsome traitor, and with your dubious remnant of a mind and your wretched morality link yourself with whomsoever you will; but never again have the effrontery to make use of our sacred language and to sully it with your vile spirit and poisonous health.*
> —FERDINAND SCHULZ
> Czech author, addressing Masaryk's involvement in the forged manuscript scandal

Masaryk, associate professor of philosophy at the Czech University of Prague, in 1882. Though he had many critics, the young professor appealed to some students because of his stimulating lectures on the British philosophers and his commitment to Czech nationalism.

One courageous doubter, a leading expert on the Czech language by the name of Ignaz Gebauer, found it difficult to get his work on the subject published, so in 1886 he turned to Masaryk. Masaryk, already a doubter, found Gebauer's work convincing and printed it in his scholarly journal. As he later explained to Karel Čapek, "To me, the question of the manuscripts was first and foremost a moral question. If they were forgeries, we must confess it before the whole world. Our pride, our culture, must not be based upon a lie."

The result was a dispute that lasted several years and embittered the entire Czech nation. Masaryk not only printed the work of scholars like Gebauer but also wrote articles attacking the manuscripts himself. As a result, much of the hatred and resentment aroused by the dispute fell on his head. He lost friends and suffered in his career. In 1886 he was denied an expected promotion from associate to full professor, and in 1888 he was officially reprimanded by the Czech University of Prague for causing dissension among his colleagues. As he told Čapek, he would overhear drinkers in bars telling how Masaryk had been paid by the Germans to belittle the Czechs and would also overhear straphangers in streetcars cursing "that traitor Masaryk."

When the dispute finally died down at the end of the 1880s, however, all but a few stubborn holdouts agreed that the manuscripts were forgeries, probably done by Hanka, the man who had claimed to have discovered them. Masaryk had become well known. Although Masaryk was not generally loved among the Czechs, at least he had made himself respected.

In addition, Masaryk's honesty and his insistence that others acknowledge the truth had won him a group of disciples and sympathizers who felt real affection and admiration for him. Every semester that he taught, a few students were impressed by his abilities as an instructor and scholar. They admired his new ideas and his knowledge of foreign cultures, respected his honest criticism of the Czech nation, and were attracted by his unusual willingness to debate major issues with them. These students stayed in touch with Masaryk after they graduated, and after 10 years, they formed a sizable group of devoted followers.

There were a few other junior professors who shared Masaryk's dissatisfaction with the cultural achievements of the Czechs and who had also been on his side in the dispute over the manuscripts. This group of allies and followers now acquired a name. Because they insisted on avoiding nationalistic illusions and false rhetoric about the achievements of the Czechs, they came to be known as the Realists. In 1887 they began to publish a weekly magazine, which enabled them to spread their ideas among educated Czechs. With this new prominence and ability to influence public opinion, a new field of activity opened for Masaryk. The professor was about to try his hand at politics.

I don't believe in a specially chosen nation. I have no need to belittle other nations in order that mine appear superior. I know the faults of other nations, but that does not cause me such pain as the faults of my own nation, which are my own faults. I gladly recognize the things in which other nations excel, but that has no influence upon my national feeling.
—TOMÁŠ MASARYK
1895

4

The Lonely Politician

Since before Masaryk was born, the main political problem for the Czechs had been how to win back the self-government that they had enjoyed as an independent kingdom during the Middle Ages. Most Czechs believed that if they were once again to take their place among the foremost European nations, they first had to achieve some kind of self-government. But this was far more easily said than done.

At the time of the National Awakening, the political leaders of the Czechs did not actually want to become independent of the Hapsburgs. They felt that as long as Hapsburg rule was not repressive, it had real advantages. Under the Hapsburgs, the Czechs belonged to an empire of 50 million people, which counted as one of the great powers of Europe. Life without the Hapsburgs, right next door to mighty Germany and not far from enormous Russia, might have been dangerous for the relatively tiny Czech nation.

A kingly man loves opposition, for opposition either strengthens him in the truth or frees him from lies.
—VAN EEDEN
Dutch poet

Masaryk's relentless insistence on telling the truth and exposing fraud made him an outcast among the Czech people. Still, he was able to garner support and win a parliamentary seat in 1891.

The emperor of Austria-Hungary, Franz Josef I (center), meets with the rulers of Russia (left) and Germany. In his stubborn effort to unify the empire, Franz Josef I sometimes tried repression and sometimes made concessions that did not go far enough to satisfy his subjects.

What most Czech leaders wanted, therefore, was self-government under Hapsburg rule. They wanted Bohemia, Moravia, and Silesia once again to form a single kingdom, with its own constitution, laws, government, parliament, and army. The ruler, however, with important powers such as appointing government leaders and commanding the army, would be none other than the Hapsburg emperor. In this way the Czechs would once again become a self-governing nation, and Austria-Hungary would remain a great power.

The Hapsburg emperor Franz Josef I would not agree to this, however, for it went against the traditional policies of his family. To hold the many peoples of the empire together, the Hapsburgs had usually relied on a powerful imperial bureaucracy, rigidly controlled from Vienna and backed up by the army. They had also given privileges to two nations in particular, the Germans in the western half of the empire and the Hungarians who lived in the eastern half, hoping to enlist their aid to hold down the others.

Between 1859 and 1866, defeat in war and mounting government debts weakened Franz Josef's power, and he was forced to make concessions.

Most of the concessions, though, went to the traditionally privileged nations. In 1867 the kingdom of Hungary, covering the entire eastern half of the empire, won exactly the kind of self-government under Hapsburg rule that the Czechs wanted. In the same year, the government of the western half of the empire, where the Czechs lived, was also reformed. A parliament was set up in Vienna to represent the western provinces, and there were local assemblies in each province, including Bohemia, Moravia, and Silesia. However, only wealthy citizens, who were more often than not Germans, were entitled to vote, and the emperor and the German-speaking imperial bureaucracy still made most of the important decisions, so that the Vienna parliament had little real power.

Having bought off the Germans and the Hungarians in this way, Franz Josef decided not to give in to the wishes of the less powerful Czechs. His decision caused bitter disappointment and resentment among the Czechs — feelings that in the long run would become a deadly threat to Austria-Hungary — but obviously the Hapsburgs were too powerful to be overthrown anytime soon. For the foreseeable future, the Czechs had to live with the ruling dynasty. How, in the face of Franz Josef's refusal to meet their wishes, were the Czechs to progress toward self-government and equality with the Germans?

The Austro-Prussian War of 1866 was a step toward the dissolution of the Austro-Hungarian empire: The Hungarians were given self-government; a parliament, which was dominated by the Germans, was set up in Vienna; and the Czechs, who were given nothing, had the seeds of rebellion planted in their heart.

In July 1867, Franz Josef I had himself crowned king of Hungary, thereby acknowledging Hungary as a self-governing state within the empire. During the late 19th century, the Czechs sought and were determined to achieve the same status for themselves.

Ever since he was old enough to take an interest in politics, Masaryk had watched the political leaders of the nation struggle to answer this question. Finally, in 1890, he decided to supply some of the answers himself. A new and increasingly popular political party called the Young Czechs had appeared. They badly needed candidates with ideas and influence over public opinion. In 1890, Masaryk joined them, and in the following year he was elected to the Vienna parliament, representing a district in Bohemia.

The Young Czechs were popular because they expressed the frustration and resentment the Czech people were feeling. They made fiery speeches praising the nation and attacking its foes, especially the Germans and the Hapsburg authorities, though they took care to show deference to the emperor himself. In many ways they encouraged just the kind of nationalistic illusions and false pride that Masaryk opposed. Masaryk was well aware of this, and he had joined the Young Czechs hoping to change their way of thinking. The only trouble was that he lacked one basic quality of a successful politician—the ability to get along with his party.

To influence the Young Czechs would have required skillful back-room politicking, and Masaryk was too blunt and forthright for that. Not long after he was elected, he made a public speech in which he said of his own party, "We proclaim our radicalism — and we don't have any clear-cut radical program." The complaint was perfectly accurate, but the party leaders did not enjoy reading in the newspapers that one of their own party members had accused them of being all talk and no action. Masaryk's relations with the party leaders went from bad to worse, and in 1893 he resigned from parliament to return to university teaching.

All the same, Masaryk continued to be interested in politics. Even if he had failed to influence the Young Czech politicians, he still hoped to influence public opinion with his teaching and writing. During the rest of the 1890s, Masaryk was busier than ever before. He edited magazines and wrote endless articles expressing his views. He published several books, with titles like *Our Present-Day Crisis* and *The Czech Question*. He continued to lecture and gain followers among students. In everything he did, he was trying in one way or another to find answers to the problems of the Czech nation. The answers he came up with were the same that he would put into practice 30 years later, as the liberator and president of Czechoslovakia, but in the 1890s most of his proposals were still unpopular.

The Vienna parliament building. In 1891, Masaryk, having joined the Young Czechs party, was elected to the Vienna parliament, where he argued for better education and greater social welfare for the Czech people.

A Moravian peasant works in the field. While in parliament, Masaryk was a staunch advocate of autonomy for the Czechs, but he was also concerned about the more immediate problems facing the Czech peasantry and the uneasy relations between the higher and lower classes among his people.

This was partly because Masaryk fought against widespread nationalistic illusions. The Czechs, he said, should stop complaining about not having self-government and instead get to work on improving themselves in practical, workable ways. He advocated improvements in education, comprehensive social welfare, and greater respect between the upper and lower classes. He implored the Czechs to settle their disputes with the Germans. Then, said Masaryk, the Germans would feel safe in giving up their privileges and would maybe even cooperate with the Czechs in winning democratic self-government from the Hapsburgs.

Masaryk also told the Czechs to give up the hope that their problems would be solved for them by a foreign power that many of them were looking to for eventual liberation: Russia. Both the Czechs and the Russians belonged to the same group of European nations, sharing related languages and the same Slavic origin. One day, many Czechs hoped, the Russian emperor, or czar, would put pressure on Franz Josef to grant their demands, or in some future war the czar would conquer Austria-Hungary and liberate the Czechs from Hapsburg rule. Masaryk, who unlike most Czechs of his time knew Russian and had visited Russia, disagreed. The Russians, he said, knew nothing about the Czechs and cared even less. The government of the czar was far too incompetent to win a major war against Austria-Hungary, and even if it did the Czechs would simply find themselves under a despotism worse than that of the Hapsburgs.

With these criticisms, Masaryk adopted the tones of a stern schoolmaster, telling his fellow Czechs to give up their quarreling and daydreams and urging them to strive for their goals with discipline and hard work. Not surprisingly, the Czech people resented being spoken to as spoiled children — particularly because Masaryk's own proposals seemed just as unrealistic as the illusions he condemned.

Masaryk was full of what looked like impractical religious idealism. He insisted that the problem the Czechs faced was not simply that of winning self-government or gaining equality with the Germans.

These things, he believed, were only part of a far bigger and nobler task — that of fulfilling their God-given destiny among the nations of the world. Although Masaryk had long ceased to be a Catholic, he remained deeply religious. He believed that God guided the entire human race — not just individuals, but also nations. "To me," he wrote, "the Czech problem involves the whole destiny of humanity. I believe . . . that the history of nations is not a matter of chance, but that in it the clear plan of Providence is revealed. It is therefore . . . the task of every nation to find out its place in this plan . . . and to proceed accordingly in all its activities, including politics."

In some ways, this was a noble and inspiring message. According to Masaryk, the destiny assigned to the Czech nation by God was to act as a beacon of religious faith, a model of upright and honest behavior, and a symbol of progress in knowledge and culture in a world that all too easily gave in to wickedness, dishonesty, and superstition. Although the Czechs composed a small nation, they had a great destiny — not just of advancement for themselves, but of service to the whole human race.

Masaryk's message, however, was also divisive and confusing. He believed that in their search to fulfill their destiny the Czechs had a great adversary — the Catholic church, which they had rebelled against in the Middle Ages and had then been forced to accept by Hapsburg persecution and repression. This idea provoked the scorn and resentment of all those who were both loyal Czechs and practicing Catholics. True, the majority of Czechs were either indifferent to religion or, like Masaryk, had turned against the church, but most of them simply could not understand why Masaryk was making such a fuss about God and religion.

Besides his idealistic talk about the destiny of the Czech nation, Masaryk had other proposals about how the Czechs should solve their problems. He strongly believed that the Czechs should try to win self-government not just for themselves but for all the unprivileged nations of Austria-Hungary. Many of these were Slav nations, like the Czechs. Their neighbors in the northern parts of the empire, the

Poles, Ukrainians, Ruthenians, and Slovaks, were all Slavs. In the southern territories of the empire, there were the Serbs, Croats, and Slovenes — the South Slavs, as they were called. Masaryk believed that as the most advanced and prosperous of Slav nations in the empire, the Czechs were bound by a duty to help their brothers. Helping them would also be to their advantage, because as part of a Slav alliance within the empire, the Czechs would have much greater bargaining power with the emperor and with the Germans.

Masaryk not only argued for this, he began forging the Slav alliance on his own. Many of his students in Prague had come from other Slav nations, and by the end of the 1890s, Masaryk had a network of former students stretching across all the Slav nations of Austria-Hungary. Some members of the network were themselves becoming political leaders.

Among the Slav nations that Masaryk began to influence in this way was the one that was closest to the Czechs in language and origins and from which he himself was partly descended — the Slovaks. Almost alone among Czech and Slovak leaders, Masaryk thought that the two nations were likely to play an important role in each other's destinies, as brothers and future partners.

The Slovaks had lived for 1,200 years in the region immediately to the east of the Czech provinces. The languages of the two nations were so similar that a Czech and a Slovak, speaking to each other in their own language — as did Masaryk's own mother and father, for instance — had little difficulty understanding each other. But the history of the two nations had been very different. The Czech territories were rich and fertile, whereas Slovakia was poor and mountainous. The Czechs had in earlier times been a leading European nation and were now on the way to recovering this position; for a thousand years, the Slovaks had been a mere subject nation of the kingdom of Hungary.

Although Hungary had now won self-government, the position of the Slovaks did not improve but was made worse. The Slovaks were only one among many non-Hungarian nations living in the kingdom

The idealism of the younger generation of Southern Slavs, the incentive to shake off the corrupt past, were the direct fruit of [Masaryk's] teaching.
—R. W. SETON WATSON
British historian and journalist, 1913

of Hungary. There were also Croats, Serbs, Romanians, and many others, amounting in all to two-thirds of the population of the kingdom. The Hungarian leaders, however, were among the most aggressively nationalistic in Europe. They had rigged the constitution, laws, and government of the kingdom so as to dominate the non-Hungarian majority that lived under their rule. In Slovakia, it was impossible to get a grade-school education or fill out a tax form without knowing Hungarian. Even privately run Slovak schools and cultural organizations were forbidden. The proclaimed intention of the Hungarian leaders was to eliminate the languages and traditions of the Slovaks, and of all the other non-Hungarian nations in the kingdom. As one Hungarian politician bluntly said, "There is no such thing as a Slovak nation."

In 1890, Masaryk began to do what he could to help the Slovaks in their struggle to survive as a nation. He started taking his family for summer vacations in Slovakia to enjoy the beauty of the mountains and to go hunting in the forests — at least until his wife convinced him to leave the animals alone. But he did not go there only to relax:

Jan Herben (seated, far left) and other Moravian and Slovak disciples of Masaryk pose for a formal portrait in the late 19th century. By the turn of the century, Masaryk had a network of such followers throughout Austria-Hungary, many of them former students who had become important political figures in their own right.

His visits enabled him to keep in touch with his Slovak ex-students and encourage them to organize against Hungarian domination.

The Hungarian police and officials, of course, knew what Masaryk was up to, and they did not like it. They could not keep him out because, as a subject of the Hapsburg emperor, Masaryk was not a foreigner in Hungary, but they did what they could to make things difficult for him. In 1893 he traveled with his wife and children to attend a wreath-laying ceremony at the birthplace of Jan Kollár, a famous poet of Slovak origin. The ceremony was interrupted by a squad of heavily armed Hungarian police, who leveled their carbines at the wreath layers and ordered them away. In a nearby inn, Masaryk scornfully told his fellow guests: "I'm a combatant in political battles, but to have a bayonet pointed at me — that I've seen only in Hungary, which is supposed to be a land of liberty!" Soon afterward, Masaryk had the chance to see the same thing again when the police raided the inn and ordered the guests to clear out.

In spite of the Hungarian police, by the end of the 1890s there were enough of Masaryk's followers to start their own magazine. In each issue they proclaimed the same ideas for Slovak readers as the Realist magazines did for the Czechs. Now both nations could hear Masaryk's message. If the Slovaks wanted to survive as a nation and liberate themselves from Hungarian domination, they needed to seek the help of their brothers, the Czechs. If the Czechs wanted to fulfill their destiny among the nations, they had to begin by helping their brothers, the Slovaks, toward enlightenment, progress, and democracy. There would arise a new combined nation, stronger than either of its separate partners — the Czechoslovak nation. It was in the 1890s, in the writings and speeches of Masaryk and his followers, that this word first came to be commonly heard.

Yet few other leaders, Slovak or Czech, liked the idea of a Czechoslovak nation. The existing Slovak leaders were a handful of educated men, struggling to keep alive the traditions and language of their nation of peasants and mountain shepherds. Most of them shared the dream of being liberated by mighty Russia. They also feared that in a partnership with the more advanced and better-educated Czechs, the Slovaks would lose their identity perhaps even faster than they would under the Hungarians.

As for the Czech leaders, they were already fighting an uphill struggle for self-government for their own nation and equality with the Germans. To them, Masaryk's call for Czechoslovak unity seemed highly unrealistic. As long as Austria-Hungary existed, the emperor, the Germans, and the Hungarians would never allow the Czechs and Slovaks to unite.

Masaryk himself knew this perfectly well. In fact, at the end of the 1890s he was coming to believe that neither the Czechs nor the Slovaks nor any other peoples of Austria-Hungary would solve their problems as long as they stayed under Hapsburg rule. Early in 1898 he wrote to a Young Czech politician about the possible end of Austria-Hungary. "I want this actually to happen," he said. "After all, such things do actually happen." But how could it happen? Masaryk had no idea. He might demolish the dreams of others, but he himself was the most unrealistic dreamer of all.

To add to Masaryk's isolation and unpopularity among the Czechs, in 1899 he again got involved in a bitter nationwide dispute in which his insistence on telling the truth once more made him widely hated.

The affair began when Masaryk undertook to prove the innocence of a homicide suspect, Leopold Hilsner, who had been sentenced to death for murdering a young peasant woman in a village in Moravia. Hilsner was a local ne'er-do-well with a history of petty crime — just the kind of person whom many people probably felt the world would be better without, whether he was guilty or not. But what made Hilsner's cause unpopular was the fact that he was Jewish and that the killing was allegedly a ritual murder. According to local gossip, Hilsner had killed the young woman in order to drain her blood and

Czech peasants pose proudly in their festive native attire. Masaryk believed that the Czechs had a great destiny — to become a prospering, independent, and influential member of the world community — and was determined to do his part to lead his people in that direction.

mix it with flour to make the Jewish Passover bread.

The belief that the Jews used Christian blood in their rituals was widespread all over central and eastern Europe. Masaryk himself, as a boy, had kept away from houses in which Jewish families lived for fear that they might kill him and take his blood. Anti-Semitism — that is, hatred and suspicion of Jews — was, however, not just a matter of village superstitions; it was a powerful political force. Many Christians tended to blame the Jews for their problems. Peasants and small businessmen who found it hard to make a living, educated people who could not find jobs they considered worthy of their talents, and Catholics and Protestants alarmed at declining respect for the churches were often anti-Semites. Consequently, politicians took up anti-Semitic ideas to win votes. Among the Czechs, political leaders who agreed on little else were all sure that Hilsner must be guilty, or that if he was innocent, it would be best to keep quiet about it. So they were all enraged and scandalized when a letter appeared in a leading Vienna newspaper explaining in detail why the whole idea of Jewish ritual murder was a wicked falsehood and anti-Semitism itself was a "disease." The signature under the letter was that of Professor T. G. Masaryk.

Masaryk followed this letter with a series of articles and pamphlets in which he revealed the many weaknesses in the evidence against Hilsner and attacked the ritual-murder superstition as well as anti-Semitism in general. Largely owing to Masaryk's efforts, Hilsner was retried. Though he was again found guilty, the original death sentence was commuted to life imprisonment, and he was eventually pardoned and released in 1918.

Enraged though they were by all of this, Masaryk's bitter opponents took comfort in the belief that by defending a Jew accused of ritual murder, Masaryk had put himself in a position where he could be destroyed politically. They devised a scheme to discredit Masaryk once and for all. At the Czech university there was a big anti-Semitic faction among the students. Masaryk's opponents planned to persuade these anti-Semitic students to crowd into Masaryk's lecture hall and shout him down. It would be a public humiliation from which he would never recover.

The disruption was well prepared. Anti-Semitic newspapers as far away as Vienna reported gleefully that "at his next lecture, Professor Masaryk will experience an unpleasant surprise." Finally the day came, and Masaryk appeared in the lecture hall with his wife, to be booed and heckled by 1,200 students. When the noise would not die down, Masaryk took a piece of chalk and wrote on the blackboard. He made a list of five points that reasserted his stand on the Hilsner case and then wrote, "I have always defended and I always will defend freedom of thought and feeling, and I won't be diplomatic about it. What do you demonstrators have against that? Explain your reasons, I'll respect them, and I'll demand respect in return." A student took up the challenge and wrote on the blackboard a statement against Masaryk, ending with the words: "Even if Hilsner had sliced [Masaryk] open, he would not have got any Czech blood from him."

The university authorities took no action against the students on account of the uproar and asked Masaryk to cancel his lectures for the rest of the week. Later, in the face of continued disruption, Masaryk had to cancel his lectures altogether. Among Masaryk's fellow professors, who one might have thought had an interest in keeping order in the lecture hall, only two openly condemned the students' action.

In the university, among the politicians, and among the Czechs, Masaryk was almost alone. All he had was his close followers and his family. On one occasion there was talk (which never came to anything) of a joint committee of Jews and Christians who opposed anti-Semitism giving him a gift of money in recognition of his work on the Hilsner case. He said he would take the money if offered and spend it on various worthy causes but added, "Some I'll keep, and I'll pack my bags and go." It was Charlotte Masaryk who persuaded her husband to stay in Prague. Very soon after the beginning of the 20th century, he found that she was right.

5

The Party Leader

Masaryk owed the turn in his fortunes mainly to his close friends and followers of the Realist group. They were sure that in spite of their leader's unpopularity there must be at least a minority among the Czechs who agreed with his ideas and respected his courage. In order to rally these supporters and perhaps add to their numbers, Masaryk's friends decided — against his own wishes and advice—to found a new political party.

The new party was officially called the Czech People's party, but it came to be more commonly known as the Realist party. It faithfully followed Masaryk's ideas on democracy and social and economic betterment, on cooperation between Czechs and Slovaks, and on self-government for every nation of Austria-Hungary. The inaugural meeting was held in March 1900, shortly after Masaryk's 50th birthday. According to his friend Jan Herben, when Masaryk arrived and saw that several hundred people had actually turned up, many from distant towns and villages, his face lit up with "the first smile that we had seen from him for a long time." All of a sudden, he saw that he had a network of supporters that spread right across the Czech territories.

> *I saw that we must be politically free if we were to go freely our own spiritual way. . . . I do not suggest that the State is the fulfillment of our cultural mission; we must prepare for the Kingdom of God that is to come.*
> —TOMÁŠ MASARYK

By 1914, Masaryk, now in his sixties, had established an international network of influential contacts and had acquired a great deal of popular support abroad, even though his reputation at home was somewhat mixed. This broad base of support was to prove invaluable to him during World War I.

Jan Herben, a close friend and associate of Masaryk's, was a writer and an outspoken advocate of Czech nationalism. His extended, detailed narratives describing Moravian peasant life are among the most important works of Czech literature.

In addition, Masaryk found that the Czech lands were not the only place where he had admirers. In the summer of 1901 he received a visit from a man whom he took, by his plain dress and modest behavior, to be one of the many people who came to him asking for money for worthy causes. To Masaryk's surprise, the visitor turned out to be an American millionaire, a manufacturer of pipe fittings in Chicago by the name of Charles R. Crane. Crane was interested in the history and culture of the Slav nations, and he had given money to the University of Chicago to set up courses in Slavic studies. He was in Europe on a business trip and had come specially to Prague to ask Masaryk to lecture in Chicago the following summer. The fee would be $2,000 — an enormous sum in those days. Masaryk might not have been popular at home, but in the United States, it seemed, he was a well-known and highly respected man.

Masaryk accepted Crane's offer and spent the summer of 1902 in the United States. Masaryk's lectures concentrated mainly on the history and civilization of the Czech nation. For his students, many of whom would someday be among the leading opinion makers of America, it was a compelling introduction to the subject. Still, he was not content only to teach. Scattered through the cities of the United States were communities of Czech and Slovak immigrants numbering several hundred thousand. Masaryk met with them and urged them to become involved in the political affairs of their homeland. Before long, Masaryk was gaining a considerable reputation in America's Czech and Slovak communities.

A few years later, in 1907, Masaryk again made an extended tour of the United States. He also visited Britain and was in touch with scholars in France, Italy, and Russia. He was building up an international network of friends and acquaintances. Later, when France, Britain, Russia, Italy, and the United States would all be at war with Austria-Hungary, Masaryk would have many supporters in these countries.

Masaryk's luck turned just at the right moment. Major political changes were taking place in Austria-Hungary, and there were growing tensions between the great powers of Europe, with which Austria-Hungary was deeply involved. If Masaryk was to do anything for the Czech and Slovak nations, now was the time.

The American industrialist Charles R. Crane was interested in Slavic culture and contributed large sums of money to help the University of Chicago establish a department of Slavic studies. In 1901, Crane offered Masaryk an opportunity to give a series of lectures at the prestigious American university, and Masaryk accepted the offer.

Within Emperor Franz Josef's territories, millions of his subjects who still did not have the right to vote were now demanding a say in politics. They were organized and led by new political parties, or mass parties, as they were often called. Unlike existing parties, such as the Young Czechs, which appealed mainly to wealthier and better-educated citizens, the mass parties concentrated on issues of concern to ordinary people.

Among the Czechs and many other peoples of Austria-Hungary, agrarian mass parties appeared, representing the interests of peasant farmers. Catholic parties gained the support of millions of practicing Catholics. The Social Democrats, who proclaimed the revolutionary beliefs of the German philosopher and economist Karl Marx, organized the blue-collar workers. The new mass parties often bitterly opposed each other, for they represented different classes of society and proclaimed different beliefs. But they all wanted the political system changed so as to give a say in politics to the millions of ordinary citizens they represented.

Two Czech immigrants arrive at Ellis Island, New York, in the early 1900s. During the summer of 1902, Masaryk lectured at the University of Chicago and visited several American cities, always venturing into the Czech and Slovak immigrant communities to speak directly with the people.

For a long time the emperor and his advisers had resisted the pressure of the mass parties, but in 1907 they made an important concession. In the western half of the empire, including the Czech territories, all adult male citizens were given the right to vote in elections to the parliament in Vienna. (In Hungary, where the Slovaks lived, the ruling politicians managed to keep the right to vote limited to a small number of educated and wealthy citizens until 1918.) For the Czechs, the new voting system meant important changes. The Young Czechs would cease to be the only leaders of the nation. They would have to make way for the mass parties.

As a believer in democracy, Masaryk welcomed the new voting system, but as a politician he knew it would probably make life harder for him. He was a professor, and his party consisted of a scattered network of well-educated professionals. Now Masaryk and the Realists would have to compete for the votes of ordinary, uneducated citizens against the big battalions of the mass parties.

In the first elections under the new system, held in 1907, Masaryk ran in his home province of Moravia. The clergy in the predominantly Catholic district all worked against him on orders from the powerful local archbishop. Masaryk's opponents used many of the rumors and half-truths of earlier years against him. An election handout of the Catholic party began, "Don't vote for Masaryk, and don't help him get elected! First he was a German, and now he pretends to be a Czech. He doesn't love his country, nor us, the sons and daughters of Czech mothers. He supported the Jew Hilsner, who shed the blood of a Christian girl, and shamed our nation before all of Europe." Masaryk worked very hard to get elected, however. He made dozens of election speeches, and when he spoke he educated his listeners, as any good professor does, without talking down to them. He narrowly won the election and once again took his seat in the parliament in Vienna. For Masaryk's party, as well, the elections were hardly a landslide. He was 1 of only 2 Realists among 74 Czech representatives, most of them So-

The German philosopher and economist Karl Marx predicted a working-class revolution whereby socialism would emerge as the world's dominant socioeconomic system. The Social Democrats, one of many new political parties in Austria-Hungary in the early 20th century, generally adhered to Marx's philosophy.

Wilhelm II, German emperor and king of Prussia, was Europe's most powerful monarch for more than 30 years. He was at the height of his power in 1914 as World War I began.

cial Democrats, Agrarians, and Catholics.

The new voting system was not nearly a solution to all of Austria-Hungary's problems, and the Vienna parliament was the scene of endless disputes. The German representatives clung to the privileged position of their nation in the western half of the empire, and the representatives of the other nations, including the Czechs, tried desperately to achieve equality. In the eastern half of the empire, the rulers of self-governing Hungary were clamping down fiercely on their restive subject peoples, including the Slovaks.

Emperor Franz Josef was aging, and his advisers were anxious. They were afraid of disloyalty among the Slavs and of uproar among the Germans and Hungarians if they introduced reforms to pacify the Slavs. They were afraid of Russia, which might try to win over the Slav nations under Hapsburg rule. Most of all, they feared the small country of Serbia, located on the southeastern border of the empire. Serbia was the national home of a small Slav people, the Serbs. But many Serbs lived outside Serbia, in Austria-Hungary. So also did the closely related Croats and Slovenes. More than anything else, the emperor's advisers feared that these South Slavs might try to secede and join Serbia.

To ward off all these threats, it seemed safest to the emperor's advisers to rely on the strength of Austria-Hungary's mighty ally, Germany. With German backing, they could safely lash out at anyone who threatened Hapsburg power — dissenting Slav subjects, Serbia, perhaps even Russia. The German emperor, Wilhelm II, and his advisers were very willing to be relied on. The more dependent Austria-Hungary was on Germany, the more power and influence Germany would have in central and eastern Europe.

In the Vienna parliament, Masaryk criticized and opposed all these policies. Though he was a splinter-group politician in a country where the leaders of even the biggest parties had little influence over government decision making, he had one advantage — his hatred for lies and deception and his determination to uphold the truth. Once again he exposed a major scandal, this time involving skulduggery committed by imperial officials in furtherance of Austria-Hungary's foreign policy aims.

The scandal began in 1909 in the middle of a major international crisis. The emperor had recently appointed a new minister of foreign affairs, Baron Alois von Aehrenthal. Aehrenthal was determined to show all possible adversaries that Austria-Hungary was still a power to be reckoned with. He had begun by taking over the territories of Bosnia and Hercegovina, which bordered on Serbia, and to which that country had a claim. Austria-Hungary and Serbia were on the brink of war, but there was one problem—Serbia was allied with Russia.

Suddenly, as the crisis reached its height, the Austro-Hungarian government began discovering evidence of Serbian-inspired subversion within its borders. Fifty-three Serb and Croat subjects of the empire were put on trial on charges of trying to organize a Serbian takeover of the South Slav–inhabited territories in Austria-Hungary. Then came even more serious accusations. In March 1909 a Vienna newspaper published an article by a well-known historian and journalist, Heinrich Friedjung, that accused various prominent Serb and Croat political leaders of belonging to a subversive organization, the headquarters of which was in the Serbian capital, Belgrade. To support his charges, Friedjung quoted from what he said were the secret records of the organization. The records also indicated that high-ranking Serbian government officials had attended the organization's meetings. If the accusations were true, then Austria-Hungary would be justified in attacking Serbia, and Russia would have no reason to help Serbia avoid punishment.

However, the accusations were soon exposed as false. In a sensational libel trial held in Vienna in December 1909, the Serb and Croat politicians named by Friedjung proved that he had been deceived by forgeries, and he withdrew his charges. All those who had been put on trial for treason were eventually acquitted or successfully appealed their convictions. Obviously the accusations against Serbia constituted a badly organized frame-up, but who had organized it?

If there was one man who was in a good position to answer this question, it was Masaryk. He was trusted by the accused Serbs and Croats, many of whom were his former students, and he had testified in their defense in the Friedjung trial. He had contacts in Belgrade as well and had persuaded Serbian officials to come to Vienna and give damning evidence against Friedjung's documents. Now he set out to discover who had forged them.

In the fall of 1910, one of the Croat politicians involved in the Friedjung trial gave Masaryk what turned out to be the decisive lead. It was a letter from a man named Vasić, who lived in Belgrade. Vasić claimed that it was he who had forged the documents used by Friedjung — and that he had done so with the help of legation officials on orders from the chief of Austria-Hungary's legation in Belgrade.

At once, Masaryk took the train to Belgrade and talked to Vasić. To prove the truth of his story, Vasić gave Masaryk what he claimed were additional forged documents that had never been sent on to Vienna. Later, when Vasić went on trial in Belgrade for endangering the interests of the Serbian state, Masaryk attended that trial too. He came to the conclusion that Vasić's story was true.

The affair provided a horrifying revelation of the way the imperial government of Austria-Hungary operated. Its diplomats had masterminded a forgery plot against a foreign government and had even taken a hand in manufacturing false documents. Then, officials of the foreign ministry in Vienna must have arranged for Friedjung to make public the contents of the forged documents. Worst of all, the purpose of this deception was to enable Austria-Hungary to inflict death and destruction on a small neighboring country.

An operation on this scale, carried out by diplomatic personnel of Austria-Hungary, must have been approved at a very high level. Behind the conspiracy there must have stood the minister of foreign affairs, Baron Aehrenthal. Such a high-ranking official of the emperor was a dangerous man to pursue, but he had framed Masaryk's students and the leaders of Slav nations friendly to the Czechs. Masaryk decided to attack him.

In a series of confrontations in parliament early in 1911, Masaryk forced Aehrenthal to admit much, though not all, of the truth. One of Aehrenthal's most important admissions was that one of the false documents that Masaryk had gotten from Vasić, and which Vasić claimed had been forged by a legation official, was in fact in that official's handwriting. By the time Masaryk finished with Aehrenthal, there was no doubt that there had been a forgery plot and that Aehrenthal had tried to cover it up. In addition, though Aehrenthal never admitted it, it was hard to believe that it was not he who had ordered the plot to begin with.

It was a remarkable achievement. Masaryk had publicly humiliated one of the emperor's highest-ranking officials and closest advisers and had exposed Austria-Hungary's plans and methods.

Surprisingly, Masaryk's victory over Aehrenthal did not win him greater political standing. His Czech rivals cried down his whole campaign against the foreign minister as mere publicity seeking. Even friendly politicians were perplexed by what one of them called "his fanatical search for the truth." At the age of 60, Masaryk remained what he had always been — a loner among politicians. He might sometimes win the respect of his nation, but he seemed to have missed the chance to lead it.

As for Masaryk himself, his victory over Aehrenthal gave him no particular satisfaction. It simply made him feel more strongly than ever that an empire that was governed in such a way did not deserve to survive. A friend who visited Masaryk about this time asked him what his thoughts were about Austria-Hungary now that he was in parliament and could see from close up how it worked. Masaryk answered angrily, "Put a stick of dynamite underneath it and blow it sky-high! That's all it deserves."

Soon Austria-Hungary would in fact be "blown sky-high." One of the dynamiters would be Masaryk himself.

6

"Go Abroad! Go Abroad!"

In June 1914, Masaryk was on vacation with his family in Germany. Like a great many other people that year, he had to cut his vacation short when it was interrupted by fateful news. While on a visit to the town of Sarajevo, in the Southern Slav districts of Austria-Hungary, the heir to the imperial throne, Archduke Franz Ferdinand, had been assassinated. This time, there was no doubt that the terrorist organization that had done the deed had unofficial links with Serbia. Although the Serbian government itself was not involved, Austria-Hungary decided to use the excuse to crush its annoying neighbor. On July 28, 1914, Austria-Hungary invaded Serbia.

The attack on Serbia brought into play a whole network of alliances, built up over many decades of rivalry and suspicion among the great powers of Europe. Serbia's ally Russia declared war on Austria-Hungary, and the allies of Russia and Austria-Hungary joined in too. Within a week nearly every

> *But today I see that even by arousing . . . hatred one becomes famous and respected. The hatred passes, but one's name remains in the people's heads.*
> —TOMÁŠ MASARYK

Masaryk was reelected to the Vienna parliament in 1913, the year he published one of his most important books, *The Spirit of Russia*. When war broke out a year later, Masaryk began to organize the movement for Czechoslovak liberation.

The assassination of Archduke Franz Ferdinand and his wife, the Countess Chotek, by a Serbian terrorist on June 28, 1914, set off the chain of events that led to World War I.

major European country was at war. The empires of Germany and Austria-Hungary — the Central Powers, as they were called — faced the Allies, a combination of the two Western powers, Britain and France, together with Russia on the east. The Central Powers were soon joined by Turkey, and six months later, Italy joined the Allied forces. Each war-making country prepared for a massive onslaught on its nearest enemy. The greatest war in history so far had begun.

Masaryk made his way back to Prague on railroads choked with trains carrying Czech soldiers to the battlefields and saw that they were depressed, sullen, and often drunk: Evidently they did not want to fight for the emperor. Back in Prague, Masaryk began to hear of shootings and hangings in the army — young Czech soldiers were being executed for desertion and insubordination. Masaryk's contempt for Hapsburg rule began to turn into bitter and consuming hatred — and also guilt. He later described his feelings in an account of his wartime career, "Our men were being punished for what I, a member of parliament, had advocated. Could I, should I, do less than the simple soldier-citizens whose anti-Austrian feelings I had encouraged?"

All of a sudden, Masaryk faced the biggest decision of his life. For years he had written and talked, at least in private, of destroying Austria-Hungary and of winning independence and unity for the Czechs and Slovaks. Now the time had come to act. There was not much that he could do at home, where he could be arrested at any time if he made trouble. The Czechs and Slovaks could only win independence if Austria-Hungary's enemies won the war. Someone would have to convince the leaders and peoples of the Allied countries that the overthrow of the Hapsburgs and the establishment of Czechoslovak independence were good things. The feeling grew in Masaryk that he was the one to do it. "Go abroad, with God's help, and get to work!" a voice inside him seemed to say. "Go abroad! Go abroad!"

If Masaryk followed that inner voice, he would be taking a tremendous gamble. He would be betting that the Allies and not the Central Powers would win the war. He would be betting that he could convince the Allies to do what he wanted. If he bet wrong and Austria-Hungary survived, then he would be an exile for the rest of his life, liable to be shot or hanged as a traitor if he ever set foot again in Austria-Hungary. He would never see his home or his family again.

Masaryk spent the first few months of the war trying to decide whether and when he should take this gamble. If the Central Powers won, would the Hapsburgs and the Germans revenge themselves on the Czechs by forever denying their hopes of equality and self-government? Did the Allies really need convincing to overthrow the Hapsburgs? Would the war last long enough to give him time to convince them? Would other Czech politicians agree to his providing them with a voice in the enemy camp? Could he find, among the politicians and his own followers, people to take on the risky role of underground contacts between him and the homeland? By the end of 1914, Masaryk had found out enough to know that the answer to all these questions was yes. It was high time to go.

Masaryk's daughter Olga. With her help, Masaryk eluded watchful passport officials and went into exile in December 1914. The following January, while in Geneva, Masaryk was informed that he would be arrested if he returned home.

Late in December 1914, Masaryk set out for Italy — still a neutral country — with his daughter Olga, under the guise of taking her to a health resort there. He did not have a visa from the Prague police permitting him to leave the country, as was required in wartime. He knew that they were getting suspicious of him, and he did not want to alert them by applying for the visa. Instead, he bluffed his way across the frontier, hopping back onto his train as it left the last station in Austria-Hungary, so as to get away from a suspicious passport official.

From Italy, Masaryk went on to Switzerland, also a neutral country and a listening post where emigrants, refugees, and spies were gathering from all over Europe. Here he would finally and definitely decide whether to stay abroad or perhaps risk one last visit home. At Geneva, in January 1915, he received a telegram from Vienna: "The book that you want is out of print, and will not be reprinted until after the war." It was a coded message from a friend with access to secret government information. It meant that if Masaryk went home, he would be arrested.

The decision to go abroad for good had been taken out of Masaryk's hands. Now there was no turning back: He had to stay where he was, in a foreign city, with no job or regular income, cut off from his family except for Olga, and having lost his right to receive protection from his government. He was a couple of months short of his 65th birthday, a time of life when most people look forward to a peaceful retirement. Instead, he had to "get to work, with God's help," to win independence and unity for the Czechs and Slovaks.

As difficult as this task would be, there were some things working in Masaryk's favor. To begin with, there was the enormous scale and ferocity of the war itself. By early 1915 the Germans, the French, and the British had fought each other to a standstill. Within a few months, the armies of Italy and Austria-Hungary would also struggle in vain to defeat each other in the Alps. In the east, Germany and Austria-Hungary faced Russia in a more mobile but still indecisive war. It was clear that the war would grind on for several years.

A long and devastating struggle was likely to help Masaryk achieve his goals. The longer the war lasted, the more time Masaryk would have to win the support of the Allies. Moreover, the greater the slaughter, the worse the Czechs and Slovaks would suffer and the readier they would be for revolt when the moment came. Above all, the total manpower, wealth, and resources of the Allies were greater than those of the Central Powers. The more devastating the war and the longer it continued, the more likely it was that the Allies would finally win.

This was not the only way in which the war seemed to be favoring Masaryk's efforts. It was also good for him that it was going badly for Russia. The Russian armies had begun the war with an attack on Austria-Hungary, hoping to defeat it before the Germans, busy with their own assault on France, could come to Austria-Hungary's help. But by the end of 1914 the Russians had been thrown back, and during 1915, Germany and Austria-Hungary were able to push their way into the dominion of the czar. It seemed less and less likely that the Czechs and Slovaks could ever win liberation with the help of Russia. Instead, they needed to look to France, Britain, and Italy, the democratic countries of the West. For decades, Masaryk had been isolated and unpopular because he did not share the warm feelings of most Czechs for the Russia of the czars.

While soldiers fought in the trenches of World War I, Masaryk worked to achieve unity between Czechs and Slovaks and to persuade the Allied governments to recognize the Czechoslovak national council, which he cofounded in January 1916.

Injured soldiers crowd a church used as a Russian field hospital on the first day of the Battle of Tannenberg in August 1914. The clash just inside their border was the Germans' first major victory on the eastern front during World War I.

Now he was being proven right. One of the disadvantages that had prevented him from being an effective leader was turning into an asset.

This was not the only one of Masaryk's prewar disadvantages that now began working in his favor. Another was his lonely position as a leader of a tiny splinter-group party. Most other leading Czech politicians belonged to big parties. Their power and influence came about because they were allied with dozens of like-minded politicians and supported by thousands of party members. Any of these politicians who openly opposed Austria-Hungary risked losing the support of his party colleagues and bringing down the wrath of the government on his followers. Even those politicians who agreed with Masaryk and were brave men found it wiser to play it safe.

Masaryk was in a different position. He had no party colleagues to disagree with and no influential position to lose. All he had was a small band of devoted followers at home and an international network of friends abroad. And these, in fact, were the greatest advantages of all. This was a war that the statesmen and generals of the most powerful countries, with all their millions of soldiers, did not know how to win. It was a war that would in the end bring great empires to disorder and destruction. From such a war, small groups of men who knew exactly what they wanted could snatch the chance to get it.

Throughout 1915 and 1916, Masaryk worked steadily to forge his friends and followers into such a group. By the end of 1916 he had succeeded. He had become the leader of a worldwide network dedicated to winning independence and unity for the Czechs and Slovaks.

Alongside Masaryk, two other men were mainly responsible for bringing this network into being. Both of them had been students under Masaryk in Prague, but otherwise their characters and careers were entirely different. Edvard Beneš was a college teacher like Masaryk, a colleague at the Czech University, who left Austria-Hungary in September 1915, one jump ahead of the police. Milan Štefánik, on the other hand, was a Slovak who had lived many years in France and who, when the war began, joined the French army as the most glamorous type of warrior in this war, a fighter-airplane pilot. Beneš, the persistent and painstaking lecturer in sociology, was the chief organizer and negotiator of the worldwide Czechoslovak network. Štefánik, the gallant "knight of the air," was its drumbeater and attention getter. Both deferred to Masaryk, the man who had given them their ideas, their inspiration, and the goal for which they fought.

For Masaryk, Beneš, and Štefánik to succeed, they had to have followers. No Allied statesman, particularly in the democratic countries of the West, would take them seriously unless they could show that they represented somebody besides themselves. But how could they show this with their homelands under harsh Hapsburg repression? There was only one way. The Czechs and Slovaks at home might have to be silent, but the Czech and Slovak emigrants abroad were free to speak. They had to speak with one voice and to call for independence and unity for both nations.

Much of what the three leaders did in 1915 and 1916 was intended to bring this about. They traveled and wrote endless letters to every city in western Europe where there was an emigrant community. They contacted sympathizers, held meetings, founded organizations, and started magazines. They settled quarrels and disputes and kept an eye

The sociologist Edvard Beneš cofounded the Czechoslovak national council with Masaryk and the astronomer turned fighter pilot Milan Štefánik. A colleague of Masaryk's at the Czech University, Beneš set up and worked out of the council's Paris headquarters.

KU PŘEDU! KU PŘEDU!

ZPÁTKY NI KROK!

VOJÁK ČESKOSLOVENSKÉ
: ARMÁDY VE FRANCII :

More than 120,000 Czechs and Slovaks fought on the Allied side against Austria-Hungary in World War I. This Czech recruitment poster reads, Forward! Forward! Backward Not a Step!

out for double agents of Austria-Hungary. Above all, they insisted over and over again that Czechs and Slovaks work together for a united and independent Czechoslovakia.

Beneš set up a headquarters organization in Paris called the National Council of the Czech Lands. Štefánik visited Russia, trying to gain the allegiance of the hundred-thousand-strong Czech community there and to combat the influence of would-be leaders who still looked to the czar for liberation. But if Masaryk, Beneš, and Štefánik were to succeed, they also had to gain the support of the largest and most distant of all Czechoslovak communities, the emigrants in the United States.

Here again, some of Masaryk's prewar activities, which had seemed politically unimportant at the time, now began to pay off. Of all the Czech politicians, he was the only one who had visited and spoken to the emigrant communities in the United States. When newspapers or returning visitors to Europe brought the news that Professor Masaryk had gone into exile and was working for the independence and unity of Czechs and Slovaks, his name and his ideas already meant something to emigrants in Chicago, Cleveland, Pittsburgh, St. Louis, and many other cities. As a result, Štefánik and other agents acting in Masaryk's name were able to get the cooperation of Czech and Slovak ethnic organizations across the United States.

The support of the American emigrants was vital to Masaryk's cause. Czech and Slovak Americans, making use of their status as citizens of a neutral country, crisscrossed war-torn Europe as couriers linking the various Czech communities, and sometimes as spies bringing information out of Austria-Hungary. Czech and Slovak ethnic organizations collected money to pay the expenses of Masaryk's worldwide network — more than $1 million by the end of the war. As a result, Masaryk never had to ask for a penny from the Allied leaders he was trying to influence. Perhaps most important of all, it was only in the United States that there existed a sizable community of emigrant Slovaks as well as Czechs. It was only with their support that Masaryk could truly claim that his organization was Czechoslovak.

As a leader representing roughly half a million Czechs and Slovaks around the world, Masaryk was someone whom the Allied leaders had to take seriously, but by itself that did not mean that they would do what he wanted. For the first two or three years of the war, most Allied leaders wanted to defeat Austria-Hungary but not to destroy it. They were afraid that if the nations under Hapsburg rule became independent, they would not be able to stand up against their powerful neighbors, Germany and Russia. The leaders of France, Britain, and Italy did not want to give their enemy Germany, or even their not-so-beloved ally Russia, a chance to dominate central and eastern Europe after the war. Therefore, they believed, it was in the interests of their countries to allow Austria-Hungary to survive.

Masaryk, of course, did not agree with this, and he wanted to change the views of the Allied leaders. However, he was a Czechoslovak, not a Frenchman, an Englishman, or an Italian. His arguments would be much more convincing coming not only from him but also from citizens, of Allied countries, who were not ethnic Slavs.

Here again, Masaryk's prewar activities now began to pay off. In all the Allied countries there were people who knew him, respected him, and shared his ideas. Some of them were university professors like himself, often specialists in the history and culture of the Slav nations. These foreign colleagues started up French- and English-language magazines and journals with titles like *The Slav World* and *The New Europe*. Others were newspapermen who had heard of Masaryk or had gotten to know him personally as a result of his sensational revelations of the forgery plot against Serbia. They were able to swing influential papers like the London *Times* and *Le Matin* behind the cause of Czechoslovak independence.

The result was that all over the Allied countries, opinion makers began proclaiming Masaryk's message. They told their fellow countrymen that it was in the interest of France, Britain, and Italy to break up Austria-Hungary because the Hapsburgs would never be more than a front for German domination of central and eastern Europe. It would be much better for the Western countries if they had several small but grateful allies in central and eastern Europe than to prop up Austria-Hungary, which claimed to be a great power but was really only a feeble satellite of Germany.

Masaryk's friends not only appealed to the interests of France, Britain, and Italy as great powers, they also appealed to their ideals as democratic countries. They argued, just as Masaryk had argued before the war, that the fate of small nations such as that of the Czechs and Slovaks was just as important to the human race as that of large ones. In

Europe, they said, every small nation must be independent and free of outside control, so as to make its unique contribution to the progress of humanity. As Masaryk said in a lecture in London late in 1915: "No master races, but national equality and parity; liberty, equality, and fraternity among nations, as among individuals. These political principles . . . are the foundations of democracy within the single nations, and they are the foundation of democratic relations between states and nations, of democratic internationalism."

Masaryk and his supporters in France, Britain, and Italy were not just calling for Czechoslovak independence. They made this part of a vision of a better future in which every nation would be equal in status and rights with every other nation, no matter how large or small its numbers, wealth, and power. To the leaders and peoples of the Allied countries looking for a reason to justify two years of slaughter and probably several more such years to come, this vision was inspiring.

The weakest links in the worldwide independence network were in the Czech and Slovak homelands. In the first two years of the war, Hapsburg rule was harshly repressive. Under emergency wartime rules, books and newspapers were strictly censored, and the police had more or less unlimited powers to keep watch on suspected subversives, search their houses, and arrest them. Those arrested came up before special army courts, staffed by officers who were suspicious of the Czechs and eager to make examples of those suspected of subversion by inflicting savage punishments on them. Several prominent politicians were convicted of treason by the army courts and sentenced to death, though the sentences were not carried out. Most other politicians —as the price of continuing to lead their parties and staying out of jail—found it best to make occasional declarations of loyalty to the Hapsburgs.

At the height of the repression, the Czechoslovak network abroad almost lost touch with the homeland altogether. Masaryk had left behind him a small group of close followers and sympathetic politicians — the Mafia, as it came to be called after the war — to act as his clandestine contacts. From time to time he managed to send them information and letters, which messengers carried across the frontier in hollowed-out umbrella handles or in packages they left in railroad baggage offices before mailing the claim check to a Mafia contact. Police surveillance was hard to evade, however, and the Mafia contact people were always afraid of penetration by double agents. On one occasion a messenger brought in, at great risk, an important letter from Masaryk, who was in Geneva. But the contact in Prague did not trust the messenger and burned the unopened letter in front of him.

All the same, the Hapsburg police never completely broke the links with the homeland. Sometimes they even strengthened these links by their own mistakes. Early in 1917 the Prague police ordered all newspapers in the province of Bohemia to publish an article accusing Masaryk of being paid by the Allies to issue statements and set up organizations in the name of the Czech nation. For many Czechs, insulated from foreign news by wartime censorship, this was the first they had heard of a movement abroad for independence led by Masaryk. As the hardships and bloodshed and repression continued and more and more Czechs came to hate the Hapsburgs, they too began to think of Masaryk as their leader.

For Masaryk, to build his worldwide network meant endless work and travel. He was forever on the move, from Switzerland to France, from France to Britain, and to countless towns and cities inside those countries — wherever there was a meeting to speak at, an emigrant community to visit, or a politician or newspaperman to whom he could talk. There were mountains of letters to read and answer and cables to and from Beneš and Štefánik, who were usually hundreds or thousands of miles away from wherever he was. There were newspaper and magazine articles to be written. In addition, in 1916, Masaryk was a professor at the University of London. British friends had gotten him this job so as to increase his standing in their country, but it also meant that he had to give regular lectures.

As there is no Superman, so there is no Super-right of great nations. The great nation has no right to use its smaller neighbors as the tools of imperialistic fancy, and of an inordinate craving for power. On the other hand, the small nations must not try to imitate the great; they must be satisfied to go their own way.
—TOMÁŠ MASARYK
1916

To master all this work took total dedication almost to the point of obsession. As Masaryk described it afterward to Karel Čapek: "It's strange. I was just like a machine that had been wound up. I had nothing in my head but our action against Austria. I could see and feel nothing else, just as if I had been hypnotized." However, even obsession could not save Masaryk from constant anxiety and fear, especially fear for his family. Early in 1915 he learned that his son Herbert had died of typhus contracted from war refugees. In the fall, he heard that his daughter Alice had been arrested and his wife had suffered a nervous breakdown. Early in 1916 he read in the newspapers that his son Jan was to be, or perhaps already had been, hanged as a traitor. It was several weeks before he found out that the report was false. It was about this time that he said to Beneš, when alone with him on an English railroad train, "I often consider whether I shouldn't go home again. Of course they'd hang me, but at least I'd get to see my wife once more."

Worst of all, perhaps, were the times when it seemed that all the hard work and anxiety were for nothing. In the fall of 1916, Edvard Beneš's brother Vojta, who was also active in the independence movement, spent an afternoon with Masaryk, walking through the streets of London. The aged emperor Franz Josef had just died. There were reports that his successor, Charles I, might try to break with Germany and make peace with the Allies. If that happened, the Czechoslovaks would never win independence. Their walk ended in a tea shop, where Masaryk began talking at length about the taxing responsibilities of leadership. Years later, Vojta Beneš wrote, "I can still see him before me — the empty teacup in front of him, his head and chest drooping across the table, his forehead a mass of wrinkles, and his trembling voice. I became aware of the grim responsibility this man had taken upon himself."

For Masaryk, leadership meant sleepless nights, loneliness, and fear. Sometimes these feelings were almost beyond endurance. But they had to be endured if Masaryk was to fulfill the responsibility he

Following the death of her son Herbert in 1915, Charlotte Garrigue Masaryk suffered a nervous breakdown. When news of her illness reached her husband in London, he was tempted to return home to be with her even though he knew he would be hanged if discovered by the authorities.

had taken upon himself of winning independence for the Czechs and Slovaks.

Fortunately for the Czechoslovak cause, the talk of peace with Austria-Hungary came to nothing; instead, in January 1917, there came a breakthrough. U.S. president Woodrow Wilson, hoping to find a way to end the war, had asked both sides to state the terms on which they would make peace. The Allies' answer listed, among other things, the liberation of the Czechs and Slovaks from foreign rule. The commitment was vaguely worded so that if the war went badly for them the Allies could get out of it without too obviously going back on their word. Still, when the war started no Allied leader would have considered going even this far. It was Beneš, the great negotiator, who had persuaded the Allies to include this among their peace conditions, building on the credit that the Czechoslovak worldwide network as a whole had gained with Allied leaders and Allied public opinion.

This was not the only change that 1917 brought for Masaryk. After a year and a half based in London, he was on the move again. Jan Herben, Masaryk's friend who was at this time a member of the Prague Mafia, described how, in April and May 1917, communications with Masaryk completely broke down,

During the early stages of World War I, the United States remained neutral, and U.S. president Woodrow Wilson acted as a mediator between Germany and the Allies. In 1916, Wilson campaigned for a second presidential term as the man who had kept the nation out of war. Soon after Wilson was reelected, however, the United States was at war with Germany.

Incompetent and stubborn, Russian czar Nicholas II was forced to abdicate the throne on March 15, 1917. He and his family were exiled to Siberia and later shot by the Bolsheviks.

and for some time the Mafia did not even know where he was. It so happened that during this time, Herben was brought in for interrogation by the Prague police. Because the interrogation was polite and he was not actually under arrest, Herben risked asking a question of his own. After all, his interrogator was a policeman, and it was his business to know things. "Where is Professor Masaryk?" Herben asked. The policeman replied, "He's in Russia. We have a press agency report that he left for Russia."

What was Masaryk doing in Russia, a country that he had always said could be of little help to the Czechs and Slovaks? In March 1917, after two years of despotic and incompetent leadership, the Russian people had risen in revolution and overthrown Czar Nicholas II. Tens of thousands of Czech and Slovak prisoners of war, captured in two years of fighting against Austria-Hungary, were now likely to be freed. Masaryk had to make sure this happened, and not just for humanitarian reasons. The freed soldiers could provide the Czechoslovak independence movement with something it badly needed. Already it had the support of Czech and Slovak emigrants, the approval of much of Allied public opinion, and the blessing of Allied leaders. Now it had the chance to build an army.

7

Daddy Masaryk

Ever since the beginning of the war, Czech and Slovak emigrants had been fighting on the Allied side, mainly as volunteers in the French Foreign Legion and in reconnaissance units in the Russian army. These Czechoslovak fighting men were few in number, but to Masaryk and his supporters, who were struggling to convince the Allies that the Czechoslovaks deserved independence, those few Czechs and Slovaks fighting on the Allied side were important. They were proof, as Masaryk put it, "that we value our freedom higher than our lives."

Meanwhile, far larger numbers of Czech and Slovak soldiers were in prisoner-of-war camps, mostly in Russia. Most of them had been unwilling soldiers of the Hapsburgs, but under the czar, they had not been allowed to fight on the Russian side. The czar's advisers and generals were afraid that they might infect the Russian soldiers with subversive Western democratic ideas.

Now that the czar had been overthrown, Russia was supposedly going to become a modern democratic country. If the Czechoslovak prisoners of war could be freed and sent into battle on the Allied side,

> *[Masaryk], who was an Austrian against his will, was engrossed by the question whether the historical moment had come when the Empire would be split up into its national ingredients. His every word and gesture conveyed his hatred for the authorities in Vienna.*
> —DR. S. SAENGER
> first German minister to the Czechoslovak Republic, 1928

Masaryk was in Russia during the 1917 Revolution. Once the czar was overthrown, Masaryk organized the newly released Czechoslovak prisoners of war and formed an army — the Czechoslovak Legion — to fight on the Allied side.

In May 1917, Aleksandr Kerensky became leader of the provisional government set up in Russia following the ouster of Nicholas II. A radical lawyer who had defended revolutionaries from persecution under the czar, Kerensky was forced out by the Bolsheviks.

that would make the Czechoslovak movement a military power in its own right. As Masaryk said to a meeting of Czech emigrants not long after he arrived in Russia, "Just imagine that we have one or two army corps at the front! Every day there will be bulletins about us, reporting on what our army is doing. Then the whole world will get to know who the Czechoslovaks are, and you can be sure they won't forget about us!"

This was the hope that brought Masaryk to Russia in May 1917. He sailed for 10 days through mine-infested waters, with a passport issued to him by the British government under the name of T. G. Marsden, in the vain hope of keeping his visit secret. Soon after Masaryk arrived in the capital city of Petrograd, however, he saw that to turn the hope into a reality would be long and difficult.

Russia was in a state of turmoil. Officially it was now a republic under a government headed by Aleksandr Kerensky, who wanted to make Russia into a democratic country like those of western Europe and to go on fighting the war against the Central Powers as a crusade for democracy. This should have made it easy for Masaryk to get what he wanted, but there was a problem: Kerensky's government was not really in control of the country. Ministers came and went rapidly in the top positions. The army generals, mostly holdovers from the czar's time, freely disobeyed government orders. Also, both Kerensky and the army generals had a menacing rival for power — the Bolsheviks, led by Vladimir Lenin.

Lenin and the Bolsheviks were seeking to create a Communist Russia, which they hoped would be the starting point for a worldwide Communist revolution. Lenin knew that after two years of fighting and dying for the czar, the Russian people were ready to lay down their arms. Kerensky called on the Russians to go on fighting, whereas Lenin promised peace and far-reaching social changes. The army generals tried to rally the soldiers for a new offensive against the Central Powers, whereas the Bolsheviks called on the soldiers to go home. Gradually, the Bolsheviks began to set up a government and army of their own, run by councils — *soviets*, in Russian — of soldiers and workers. Month by month, the soviets became more powerful and the provisional government and the official army grew weaker.

Masaryk disliked the Bolsheviks and opposed their plan for a Communist Russia, but he could see that they had the power to plunge the country into chaos and paralyze its war effort against the Central Powers. This made him finally decide on a daring plan that he had been considering already before he arrived. Somehow he must get the Czechoslovak army out of Russia, to fight alongside the French, British, and Italians in the West.

Vladimir Ilich Lenin, Communist theorist and Russian revolutionary, dedicates a monument to the German social and political philosopher Karl Marx before a Moscow crowd on November 7, 1918. A man of powerful intellect and fervent commitment, Lenin organized the Bolsheviks and created the world's first Communist state — the Soviet Union.

Masaryk, leader of the Czechoslovak Legion, addresses an audience in the Ukraine in 1917. By that fall, the legion had grown to 40,000 strong.

Meanwhile, just building the army was difficult enough. He had endless visits and discussions with overworked and indecisive officials of Kerensky's government, trying to persuade them to issue the necessary orders. Then there were further meetings with suspicious ex-czarist generals, trying to persuade them to obey the orders the government had issued. After nearly 2 months, all he had achieved was to receive permission for existing Czechoslovak troops in the Russian army to operate not in small reconnaissance groups, as before, but as a single 3,500-man brigade.

Then, on July 2, 1917, the brigade went into action. At Zborov in the Ukraine, the southwestern region of European Russia, it attacked and destroyed a 12,000-man Austro-Hungarian force. In Petrograd, 900 miles away, sitting in the editorial office of a Czechoslovak magazine publisher while the staff sang songs and danced on the tables in celebration, Masaryk wrote out a cable to Beneš and Štefánik telling them the good news. The Czechoslovaks, fighting for the first time as a united force on the Allied side, had defeated an army of the Hapsburgs.

The Russian government and generals were impressed, especially because their own army was by now hardly more than a mob of mutineers and deserters. The gates of the prison camps finally opened. Thousands upon thousands of Czech and Slovak soldiers marched out, to reassemble in barracks and training depots around Kiev, the chief city of the Ukraine. A new army — the Czechoslovak Legion, as it was called—was in the making.

This did not mean that Masaryk's work in Russia was finished. The soldiers, at first little more than huge crowds of freed prisoners, had to be organized into an army. Officers had to be selected, discipline enforced, and food and weapons procured. Above all, the thousands of young men, just released from demoralizing captivity, far from their homes and families, and unsure of what would happen to them in a country that was falling to pieces around them, needed to know that they had a cause worth fighting for and a leader on whom they could rely. Masaryk had to inspire them with the greatness of the cause and win their loyalty.

Masaryk spent much of the late summer and early fall of 1917 in the Ukraine. He inspected camps, barracks, and hospitals; he took the salute at parades; and above all, he inspired the soldiers. Masaryk was no swashbuckling warrior or fiery battlefield orator but a dignified elderly professor who spoke to them, as one soldier put it, "with mathematical calm and shorthand brevity." He made sure they were armed and fed and looked after, and he reassured them with his calm resolve. The soldiers showed their feelings for him by giving him the nickname Daddy Masaryk. To these young men, whom the fortunes of war had cast adrift from any normal life, Masaryk was indeed a kind of father.

By the fall of 1917 the Czechoslovak Legion, now an organized force of 40,000 men, united around Masaryk as its leader. It was just in time. After months of preparation, the Bolsheviks began the great revolution that would turn Russia into the world's first Communist state. On November 7, 1917, in Petrograd, Moscow, and other cities, their forces attacked the offices and military strongholds

"Daddy" Masaryk with members of the Czechoslovak Legion. The Republic of Czechoslovakia was declared on October 28, 1918, and Masaryk returned to Prague as its president.

of the government. Within a few days, they had taken over. By the end of the month, they had obtained a cease-fire from the Central Powers, to be followed by peace negotiations.

For Masaryk, the days of the Bolshevik revolution were a dangerous time. No one was shooting at him personally, but wherever he went, in Petrograd, Moscow, or Kiev, he got caught in the cross fire. The worst time was in Moscow, when the hotel in which he was staying, the Metropol, became the scene of an epic six-day battle, complete with heavy artillery, between the Bolsheviks and troops loyal to Kerensky. At the height of the battle, Masaryk crawled through the hotel lobby, bullets whizzing above his head, to get to a telephone to let the local Czechoslovaks know where he was.

With the Bolsheviks asking the Central Powers for peace, it was clear that Russia was out of the war. In the Ukraine, where the legion was stationed, local leaders proclaimed independence from Russia, and fierce fighting started between their forces and those of the Bolsheviks. Masaryk kept the legion strictly neutral in this conflict, but he knew that sooner or later there would be trouble with one side or the other. In any case, the German army, claiming to act in support of Ukrainian independence, was moving in from the west. On their own, the Czechoslovaks could not stand up against the Germans. It was urgent that the legion get out of Russia and head to the safety of the West.

To the west and south, the way to safety was blocked by Germany, Austria-Hungary, and Turkey. The northern route — to Russian ports on the Arctic Ocean, from where it would be possible to travel to western Europe by ship — meant crossing in front of the advancing German armies and then sailing through waters infested with German U-boats. That left only one way out: The legion had to travel eastward and cross the vast forests of Siberia on the world's longest railroad, the Trans-Siberian, until it arrived at the last stop, Vladivostok, 5,000 miles away on the Pacific Ocean. There it would find ships to carry it 8,000 miles back again, all the way to France.

> *The pages of history recall scarcely any parallel episode at once so romantic in character and so extensive in scale.*
>
> —WINSTON CHURCHILL
> on the Czech Legion's
> trans-Siberian trek

In the early months of 1918, the Czechoslovak Legion prepared for the first leg of its journey to Europe. On March 3, it marched off eastward while rearguard units held off the Germans arriving from the west. The Bolsheviks were cooperative. They were glad to see a possible enemy go. The Soviet of People's Commissars, the ruling group of the Bolshevik government, cabled orders to local soviets in Siberia to give the Czechoslovaks every assistance on their journey. The telegram was personally signed by a high-ranking Bolshevik leader, none other than People's Commissar Joseph Stalin.

Masaryk, however, was not with the legion. He went on ahead, traveling for three weeks in a train with no sleeping car and spending every night on a mattress stretched out on a wooden bench. He had to make sure that when the legion arrived in Vladivostok there would be ships ready to take the soldiers to Europe. In addition, there was important work for him elsewhere: In April 1917 the United States had entered the war on the Allied side, and Masaryk set his sights on making sure that the power of the world's largest democratic country would be used in the service of the Czechoslovak cause. So, when Masaryk reached Vladivostok he did not end his journey. He continued eastward, across the Pacific Ocean, until he reached America.

A trainload of Czech troops prepares to embark on a long journey from Russia to the battlefields of Europe via the Trans-Siberian Railroad in 1918. Masaryk traveled ahead of the troops in order to make arrangements for their transport.

8

"You . . . Are to Return Home Immediately"

On April 17, 1918, a telegram arrived at the Chicago headquarters of a nationwide Czech ethnic organization, the Czech National Alliance. It was from the wartime cable censorship office in San Francisco. The censors had intercepted a message to the alliance from Tokyo, Japan, stating that someone by the name of Tarsden was on his way to the United States. The censors were suspicious. "Who is Tarsden?" they wanted to know. For the alliance officials in Chicago, the censors' query was joyful news. "Tarsden," they realized, must be a garbled version of "T. G. Marsden." Masaryk was coming.

When Masaryk arrived in Chicago on May 4, the city's Czech community — the second largest of any city in the world — came out to greet him. No less than 100,000 people cheered him as he rode from the railroad station to his hotel. Chicago was not the only place where Masaryk was received in triumph. In New York, Boston, Cleveland, and Pittsburgh it was the same. Everywhere there were cheering crowds, ethnic organizations with their banners and old-country costumes, speeches and receptions, and handshakes with mayors, congressmen, and senators.

Isn't this a great world? And its biggest romance is not even . . . that Woodrow Wilson rules it, but the march of the Czechoslovaks across 5,000 miles of Russian Asia — an army on foreign soil, without a Government, without a span of territory, that is recognized as a nation.
—F. K. LANE
home secretary of President Woodrow Wilson's administration

When Masaryk arrived in Chicago on May 4, 1918, he was greeted by throngs of admirers. During his visit to the United States he took a month-long tour and met several times with U.S. president Woodrow Wilson in Washington.

Masaryk did not feel comfortable in the role of a conquering hero, but he knew he had to play the part. In his own story of the war years, he wrote, "Before the war I used to denounce 'flag-wagging,' but in America I realized that I had gone too far in criticizing it. Professor that I was then, I had failed to see that a well-organized procession may be worth quite as much as a supposedly world-shaking political article or a speech in parliament." In fact, the cheering and processions in city after city were not just a chance for Czech and Slovak Americans to greet their leader. They also had a political purpose: They were deliberately organized by ethnic leaders to show their unity behind Masaryk and his program and to display their control of large numbers of Czech and Slovak ethnic voters. All this was intended to impress politicians and officials in the last city on Masaryk's month-long tour — Washington, D.C. Above all, it was intended to get the attention of the most important official and politician of them all, President Woodrow Wilson.

The U.S. president and Masaryk had many things in common. Both had been professors before entering politics, and both saw the war as a crusade for a more democratic world in which large and small nations would live peaceably side by side.

On a stark World War I battlefield in France, American soldiers, or doughboys as they were called, fire on a German position. U.S. president Wilson declared that America's goal in the war was "to make the world safe for democracy."

However, Wilson saw the war mainly as a matter of defeating Germany, and he lacked Masaryk's bitter hatred of Austria-Hungary. In fact, Wilson's blueprint for the postwar world — his Fourteen Points, issued in January 1918 — made it clear that although the Hapsburgs would have to grant much more freedom to their subject nations than ever before, Austria-Hungary should continue to exist. Masaryk, of course, did not agree. He did not believe that the Hapsburgs would ever sincerely reform, and he had come to Washington to change Wilson's mind.

His campaign to persuade the president was skillfully conducted. He arrived in Washington not as just another foreign exile trying to get the president's ear but as the acknowledged leader of several hundred thousand Czechoslovak-American voters. Once in the capital, he made use of friendships and contacts, some dating as far back as his 1902 visit, to gain access to powerful heads of congressional committees, Allied ambassadors, State Department officials, presidents of universities, bankers, and lawyers. In this way, he was able to acquire enough influence to gain repeated access to the president and his advisers.

Masaryk had been an admirer of the United States all his life, and this, too, helped his cause. One of the first things he did when he arrived in Washington was to pay a visit to the battlefield of Gettysburg.

In October 1918, Masaryk (center, seated in large chair) visits Independence Hall in Philadelphia, Pennsylvania. He is surrounded by members of the Congress of Representatives of the Subject Races of Germany and Austria, of which he was president.

He repeatedly proclaimed that the Czechoslovak fight against the Hapsburgs was just like the American struggle against George III and that the future Czechoslovakia would be a "government of the people, by the people, and for the people," just like the United States. As a result, he won the sympathy and respect of the politicians, the president, and public opinion in general.

Meanwhile, there was something else working in Masaryk's favor: the Czechoslovak Legion, which he had left behind him in Russia. In Siberia in May 1918, the cooperation between the Czechoslovaks and the Bolsheviks broke down, and fighting started. The units of the legion, by this time strung out along the entire 5,000 miles of the Trans-Siberian Railroad, seized control of it and held it against repeated Bolshevik attacks. Thus, an Allied army now controlled the only transportation route in the Asian part of Russia. To the Allied leaders it was vital to keep the Germans out of Siberia, and they were also thinking of sending armies to crush the Bolsheviks. By seizing the railroad, the legion had done an important service for the Allies.

Gradually, Masaryk was able to persuade Wilson to favor Czechoslovak independence. On September 3, 1918, the United States recognized the National Council of the Czech Lands as a government fighting on the Allied side and thereby acknowledged that Czechs and Slovaks were struggling on the Allied side to achieve their independence. Meanwhile, in Europe, Beneš was making use of the army in Russia to win similar backing from France, Britain, and Italy. By the fall of 1918, Masaryk, Beneš, and Štefánik were no longer mere exiles pleading their case to the Allied leaders. They were Allied leaders themselves.

These successes came exactly at the right time. By September 1918, the Central Powers were losing the war. In spite of the success of Germany and Austria-Hungary in forcing Russia out of the war in 1917, they had been gradually worn down by the greater resources of the Allies. In 1917 the Germans had tried to cut off the Allies from their worldwide resources by turning their U-boats loose in the At-

Soldiers, like children, must be treated with fairness, frankness, openness; because they must obey even if it means their death, the man whom they obey must really win their respect and without hypocrisy. Military parades are, in fact, much more for the soldiers than for the officers. I like soldiers, even though I don't like war.

—TOMÁŠ MASARYK

lantic Ocean so as to starve Britain and France into surrender, but the British navy had fought off the U-boats, and the result had simply been to bring the United States into the war on the Allied side. By the summer of 1918 a million-strong American army had joined the Allied armies in France. There and on every other war front, the armies of the Central Powers were in retreat. Their soldiers were losing the will to fight, and the civilians at home were starving. Afraid that defeat might lead to communism as it had in Russia the year before, in October 1918 the leaders of Germany and Austria-Hungary asked President Wilson to arrange peace talks.

By that time, the Czech subjects of the Hapsburg emperor were ready to revolt. With the war going against them, in 1917 and 1918, Emperor Charles I and his advisers had eased the repression against the Czechs, but it was too late. The people were infuriated by hunger and bloodshed. News of the successes of Masaryk, Beneš, and Štefánik spread widely. The politicians sensed that now was the time to drop their caution, and they began to issue public statements that all but openly called for independence. After the paralysis of the early war years, a sense of power and solidarity gripped the Czechs,

A German submarine approaches a civilian steamer in the North Sea. In 1917, Germany used its U-boats in an attempt to cut off supplies to Allied forces. The threat to U.S. shipping was one factor that drew the United States into the war.

During his visit to Washington, D.C., in 1918, Masaryk is flanked by the Czech National Alliance official Charles Pergler (left) and military attaché Captain V. S. Hurban.

which they were not afraid to show publicly. In January 1918, 60,000 blue-collar workers demonstrated in Prague for peace and bread. In April another huge gathering took a solemn oath of loyalty to the nation, an oath that ended with the fateful words, "We shall endure until our nation's freedom is in our grasp." In May, Slovak leaders in Hungary, where repression was still effective, managed all the same to issue a public statement calling for free choice of government for their nation.

Finally, in July 1918, Czech politicians from all parties formed the National Committee — a kind of shadow government to prepare for independence. Through the Prague Mafia, the National Committee had clandestine links to the National Council of the Czech Lands office in Geneva. It was essential that the two agencies work closely together, for it was the exiles, not the home politicians, who had the ear of the victorious Allies.

The Allies had accepted Masaryk's program, and the events of the war years had proven him right; therefore the politicians in Prague had to accept his program as well. Together with the Slovak leaders, they had to work for a united country of both nations, governed as a democratic republic and look to the Western countries, not to Russia, for inspiration and support. The ideas of the maverick prewar politician had become the program of the Czech and Slovak nations.

The month of October 1918 was an anxious time for Masaryk. Germany and Austria-Hungary had approached Wilson rather than the other Allied leaders because they hoped that he would be more merciful to them, and this possibility worried Masaryk. On October 19, however, Wilson replied to Austria-Hungary. His message declared that it was up to the peoples of Austria-Hungary, not himself as U.S. president, to "be the judges of what actions on the part of the Austro-Hungarian government will satisfy their aspirations." By this time, there was no doubt about what action the peoples of Austria-Hungary wanted the government to take: They wanted it to disappear.

During the couple of weeks after the U.S. president had proclaimed its doom, the 400-year-old Hapsburg Empire fell to pieces. Every nation, even the Germans and the Hungarians, proclaimed its

After spending nearly four years in exile, Masaryk began his long journey home on November 20, 1918. Now his homeland was an independent Czechoslovak state, and Masaryk would be called on to provide the leadership necessary to build the new republic.

Ceded by Germany after Allied victory in 1918		Ceded by Bulgaria
Ceded by Austria-Hungary after Allied victory		Allied-occupied Rhineland
Ceded by Russia		Territories kept or ceded according to plebiscites conducted by League of Nations 1920–1922

independence, and the emperor went into exile. In the turmoil, it was hard for Masaryk to find out what was going on in Prague. Finally, in November, he received cables from Beneš and read newspaper reports that told him what had happened there. On October 28, by good organization, swift action, and skillful use of bluff, the National Committee had taken over the government from the Hapsburg officials. A delegation of the National Committee had gone to Geneva to meet with the National Council. They had agreed that Czechoslovakia should be a republic modeled after France, with a president as head of state and a prime minister to run the government. The prime minister was to be Karel Kramář, a leading prewar politician whose standing among the Czechs was very high, particularly since he had spent many months of the war in a Hapsburg jail under sentence of death. As for president, there was only one man who had the standing and authority among both the Czechs and Slovaks, and also with the Allies, to hold together the infant state of Czechoslovakia during the difficult period that lay ahead. Beneš's cable to Masaryk informing him of the decisions of the Geneva meeting contained a directive for him personally: "You, as President of the Republic, are to return home immediately."

On November 20, 1918, in New York City, Masaryk boarded a Cunard liner bound for Europe. A month later he was in Prague, receiving the most triumphant of all the welcomes that he had been given that year. It was a historic moment in the life of the Czech nation. What were his thoughts as he drove to Prague Castle as the returning hero of the nation that had so often rejected and hated him? In his own story of the war years, Masaryk answered the question himself: "The heavy work awaiting me, the work of building up our restored state decently and well, constantly weighed on my mind." Masaryk's dream of an independent Czechoslovak state had come true. But that was only the first part of his dream. Now Czechoslovakia had to be made into a country where both Czechs and Slovaks could fulfill their destinies.

What I like about America is the frankness of the people. . . . Your American racketeer is completely ruthless; he is frankly a plunderer without any pretext. . . . The good ones are equally energetic about all they consider good. . . . They are more enterprisingly good than we. There is a pioneering element about it which is in keeping with their untamed soil.
—TOMÁŠ MASARYK

9

The President-Liberator

In territory, population, and resources, Czechoslovakia was almost exactly the country that Masaryk had hoped for. It extended for 500 miles, from the frontiers of Germany to those of Russia. It had a land area of about 50,000 square miles, roughly the same as that of the state of Alabama. Approximately 13 million people lived within its borders, making it one of the smaller European countries. The Czech provinces, however, were among the industrial powerhouses of Europe, producing coal, iron, glass, leather, textiles, automobiles, and weapons. Their population was as well educated and highly skilled as any in Europe. After centuries of Hungarian exploitation, the Slovaks were still mostly a nation of peasants, with a high rate of illiteracy and emigration. Still, the Slovak mountains were rich in timber, minerals, and water power, and the Slovak peasants were hardy, persistent, and steadfast.

The problem is whether the big peoples which have hitherto threatened the small peoples and each other will accept the principle that all nations, big and small, are equally entitled to their own individualities in political organization and in culture.
—TOMÁŠ MASARYK
1925

Masaryk, the first president of Czechoslovakia, in front of his official residence in Prague. The struggle for independence had been a long and difficult one for Masaryk and his people. Now that freedom was won, the road that lay ahead promised to be just as arduous.

95

Masaryk believed that although Czechoslovakia was a small country, it was an experiment in national partnership in which all humanity had a stake. The Czechs, he believed, had to learn self-confidence and political wisdom and the Slovaks had to develop their human and economic resources if Czechoslovakia was to become a true modern nation. In partnership with each other, Masaryk declared, the Czechs and Slovaks must give the world an example of how nations could mature and progress and live unselfishly side by side.

Masaryk knew very well that making the experiment succeed would take time and work. "Often, almost every day," he told Karel Čapek, "I say to myself: Thirty years more of peaceful, sensible, energetic development, and our state will be secure." This could not be taken for granted, however. Following a terrible war and a revolutionary change of government, the list of problems that Czechoslovakia faced was a long one. The country was plagued by internal disputes and resentments both old and new. Among the Czechs, the mass parties that had arisen before the war — the Social Democrats, Agrarians, and Catholics — represented groups of voters with opposing interests and beliefs that were constantly and viciously at odds. The leaders of these parties had made their careers in the old empire, where the emperor and his advisers made all the important decisions, and they had no experience in working together to run a country.

Among the Slovaks, a tiny handful of leaders eagerly competed for political rewards that under the Hungarians they had never had a chance of gaining — government jobs and patronage, the acclaim of the people, and a chance to decide the destiny of their nation. Inevitably this led to bitter feuding, especially between those who wanted a closer partnership with the Czechs and those who wanted a looser one. In June 1918, Czech and Slovak organizations in the United States had reached an agreement, known as the Pittsburgh Agreement and signed by Masaryk as a witness, that Slovakia would have self-governing status in the future country of the Czechs and Slovaks. But in the first years

> *In the world as it is today can we keep permanently the independence we have won? Are we capable, intelligent, prudent, determined and tenacious enough to keep it?*
> —TOMÁŠ MASARYK
> questioning the staying power of the October 28 Revolution

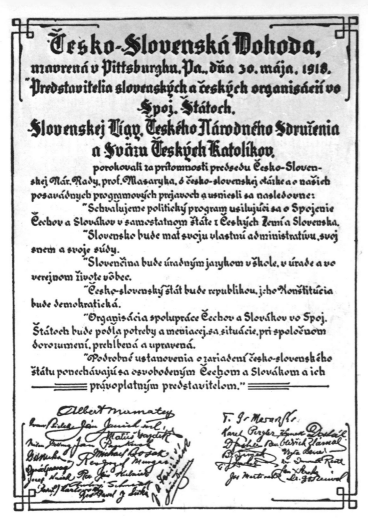

Česko-Slovenská Dohoda,
uzavrená v Pittsburghu, Pa., dňa 30. mája, 1918.

"Predstavitelia slovenských a českých organisácií vo
Spoj. Štátoch,
Slovenskej Ligy, Českého Národného Sdruženia
a Sväzu Českých Katolíkov,

porokovali za prítomnosti predsedu Česko-Sloven-
skej Nár. Rady, prof. Masaryka, o česko-slovenskej otázke a o našich
posavádnych programových prejavoch a usniesli sa nasledovne:

"Schvalujeme politický program usilujúci sa o Spojenie
Čechov a Slovákov v samostatnom štáte z Českých Zemí a Slovenska.

"Slovensko bude mať svoju vlastnú administratívu, svoj
snem a svoje súdy.

"Slovenčina bude úradným jazykom v škole, v úrade a vo
verejnom živote vôbec.

"Česko-slovenský štát bude republikou, jeho Konštitúcia
bude demokratická.

"Organisácia spolupráce Čechov a Slovákov vo Spoj.
Štátoch bude podľa potreby a meniacej sa situácie, pri spoločnom
dorozumení, prehlbená a upravená.

"Podrobné ustanovenia o zariadení česko-slovenského
štátu ponechávajú sa osvobodeným Čechom a Slovákom a ich
právoplatným predstaviteľom."

The Pittsburgh Agreement between the United States and representatives of the future Czechoslovak state was signed by Masaryk (right column, top line) in the spring of 1918. The document had no official status, but it was nonetheless an important step in the process of achieving international recognition of Czechoslovakia.

after the war, the believers in close partnership with the Czechs were running Slovakia, and Slovakia did not get the status of a self-governing province. As a result, their rivals accused them of betraying the interests of the nation. The one Slovak who might have settled these differences was dead. Štefánik was killed in a plane crash when returning home in 1919.

The various rivals in these Czech and Slovak disputes did at least want Czechoslovakia to succeed, but there were others in the new country who did not. In Slovakia, there lived 750,000 Hungarians, and in Bohemia, Moravia, and Silesia there were 3 million Germans. The Paris Peace Conference of 1919 had awarded these areas to Czechoslovakia, because without them the country could not be defended in wartime and would not be economically viable in peacetime. However, because the Germans and the Hungarians belonged to Czechoslovakia against their will, their leaders were more interested in protesting against the new country than in making it work.

The same was true of another group that developed as a major political force in Czechoslovakia soon after the end of the war — the Communists. In Czechoslovakia, as in other countries, the Communists consisted of the local supporters and admirers of the Bolshevik revolution in Russia. At first, they hoped that the Russian revolution would be followed by an immediate worldwide revolution that would sweep Czechoslovakia along with every other country. When that did not happen, they organized for a long-term struggle. For them, the goal of a peaceful and democratic Czechoslovakia without a communist revolution was a sham.

As president, Masaryk faced a new test of his leadership. He had always been a member of the opposition, undermining the authority of the Hapsburg government and finally helping to overthrow it. Now he was the government, and it was up to him to defend its authority. Masaryk had always been a loner, criticizing the political leaders of the Czech nation. Now, as president of a democratic country, he had to cooperate with the politicians to make it work.

Masaryk did surprisingly well in this unaccustomed role. He relied heavily on his scattered network of loyal followers and devoted supporters. Many members of this postwar network came from Masaryk's prewar Realist and wartime Mafia networks. Now, however, they held top positions in the government and in the leadership of different political parties, both Czech and Slovak. They also acquired a new name, the Castle, because they all responded to the orders that came down from the president's office in Prague Castle. Politicians defied the power of the Castle at their own peril. For example, Charles Pergler, a Czech American who returned after the war and went into politics, found this out the hard way. When he began attacking the Castle, bureaucrats at the passport office suddenly developed an interest in his credentials as a Czechoslovak citizen. They decided that he was really an American and ordered him out of the country.

Masaryk did not always resort to power politics to get his way. He even learned to cooperate with people who were not his close and devoted followers. For most of the 1920s, for instance, he worked closely with a group of influential politicians from several different parties — "the Fivesome," as they were called — to promote cooperation between these parties. Masaryk's closest ally in the Fivesome was Antonín Švehla, the leader of the powerful Agrarian party. Švehla was a shrewd peasant who had made his way in politics by wheeling, dealing, backslapping, and by never quarreling with anyone. During the war he had played a dangerous double game of making the necessary statements of loyalty to the Hapsburgs while also working with the illegal Mafia. Though of quite a different temperament, Masaryk respected Švehla more than he did any other politician. The combination of Masaryk the national hero, Švehla the political fixer, and the other influential members of the Fivesome did much to keep the quarrelsome politicians working together.

For the ordinary people, divided as they were by class and nation, one of the few things they had in common was love and admiration for the president-liberator, as he was officially called. In Czechoslovakia after the war, a kind of cult grew up around Masaryk. The story of his wartime feats was told and retold. His followers extolled him not just as a national leader but as a scholar, a religious thinker, and above all as a philosopher, so that he acquired the image of a philosopher-president. Following the death of his wife in 1923, books and press reports described his life of lonely dedication to the nation's service. Masaryk often made journeys around the country to show himself to the people and be cheered and greeted by them. Folksy stories were sometimes told about these trips. In his hometown of Hodonín, it was said, he recognized an old peasant woman who had been one of his playmates 70 years before. "Do you remember how we used to misbehave in church on Sundays?" he asked her. "Yes," she replied. "And do you remember how we

President Masaryk (left) and Foreign Minister Beneš. During the 1920s, Beneš helped form the Little Entente — an alliance that included Czechoslovakia, Romania, and Yugoslavia — in order to guard against a possible Hapsburg restoration in Central Europe.

used to get it on the rear end afterwards?" It was the kind of human touch that made the president-liberator seem all the more lovable. For the young Czechoslovak nation, Masaryk became what he had been for the young soldiers of the legion in Russia: Daddy Masaryk.

Under Masaryk's guidance, Czechoslovakia became one of the best-working democracies in Europe. In other European democracies quarrels between politicians often prevented the government from making decisions, but Czechoslovak democracy got things done. Its politicians, in spite of their disagreements, passed many controversial and far-reaching reforms, including painful economic stabilization measures just after the war, legislation to break up the vast landholdings of the German-speaking nobles, and comprehensive social welfare programs.

The partnership between the Czechs and the Slovaks worked too, though there was always friction. The Czechs tended to treat the Slovaks as junior partners, and the Slovaks resented this. Still, the government poured money into Slovak schools, enabling the Slovaks to become more literate and to acquire a sizable educated class for the first time in their history. Slovaks also came to wield national power. One prominent Slovak leader, Milan Hodža, eventually became prime minister.

Czechoslovak democracy even exerted a positive influence on those who did not want to be part of it. Political and national minorities slowly began to cooperate, and even when they did not, they were generally tolerated. In 1920 the government broke a Communist-organized nationwide strike by ordering systematic mass arrests, but the Communists continued to operate as a legal political party.

In all these ways, the Czechoslovak experiment was successful at home, but its ultimate success required peace and security abroad. During the war, doubters in Allied countries had predicted that if the Czechs and Slovaks won independence they would end up as mere playthings of the great powers and that sooner or later, either Germany or Russia would turn them into satellites, or perhaps even swallow them up. Masaryk was determined to prove the doubters wrong. In fact, he considered this his most vital task as president and shared it with the one man whom he trusted more than any other — the minister of foreign affairs, Edvard Beneš. Between them, Masaryk and Beneš strove to build for Czechoslovakia a strong European power position, bolstered by reliable international friendships and alliances.

Masaryk on horseback in Prague. The Masaryk presidency saw numerous economic reforms and drastic changes in the parliamentary leadership. On the international front, an important alliance was formed with France in anticipation of a resurgence of German nationalism.

In June 1931, the Little Entente convened at Masaryk's summer residence in Lany, near Prague. Here the president (center) meets with Yugoslavian foreign minister Bogoljub Jevtić (left) and Romanian foreign minister Nicolae Titulescu.

To achieve this aim, Masaryk and Beneš relied partly on the same policies that Masaryk had called upon the Czechs to follow ever since the 1890s. In those days he had advised the Czechs to cooperate with other subject nations of the empire and warned them against unnecessary feuding with the Germans. Czechoslovakia now found allies in two nearby countries of former subject peoples — Yugoslavia and Romania — forming an alliance called the Little Entente. Czechoslovakia also made great efforts to reconcile with defeated enemies, above all with the Germans: It gave economic aid to the poverty-stricken new republic of Austria, carved out of the German-speaking territories of the old empire, and helped settle bitter postwar disputes between Germany and France.

Also in the interest of national security, Masaryk took personal charge of building the Czechoslovak army into the most formidable military force in Central Europe, backed by the country's large modern weapons industry. Beneš made sure that Czechoslovakia was an upstanding member of the League of Nations, the postwar international organization that was supposed to further the cause of democracy internationally and to deter aggressors by mobilizing the united force of all its members against them. Most important of all, Czechoslovakia was allied with the Western democratic country that in the postwar world had the strongest army in Europe — France.

With this combination of alliances, international support, and military power, Czechoslovakia was one of the best-protected small countries in Europe. However, there were dangers that would not go away and gaps in the defenses that could not be filled. Among the new country's defeated enemies, the proud Hungarians refused to accept their loss of people and territory to the Slovaks. To the north, another new country, Poland, had claims on a district in the province of Silesia where many Poles lived. Of the great powers that had helped Czechoslovakia win independence, the United States had withdrawn into isolation from European affairs. The British, intent on preserving their worldwide empire, were losing interest in Central and Eastern Europe. Italy had fallen under the rule of a Fascist dictator, Benito Mussolini. Even France, exhausted by its enormous wartime losses, was likely to prove a wavering ally.

Then, in 1933, another dictator came to power. The weak German democracy was swept aside by the Nazis under Adolf Hitler. Czechoslovakia's western neighbor was about to regain its strength and become a ruthless enemy.

Adolf Hitler (fourth from right) became chancellor of Germany in January 1933. That country's troubled postwar era came to an end as Hitler revived the German economy and created a potent Nazi war machine.

On December 14, 1935, after 17 years as Czechoslovakia's head of state and having passed his 85th birthday, Masaryk resigned. He was succeeded as president by Edvard Beneš. Masaryk died on September 14, 1937. A week later, his coffin was carried from Prague Castle, through crowds that knelt and wept in the streets, back to the main railroad station to be buried beside his wife in a Protestant country churchyard.

A year after Masaryk died, his life's work fell to pieces. Hitler demanded that Czechoslovakia surrender its German-speaking areas. The mainstay of Czechoslovakia's defenses, its friendship with the Western democracies, failed. Afraid of a new war with Germany, Britain and France forced Czechoslovakia to comply with Hitler's demands. In September 1938, by the terms of the Munich Agreement, Czechoslovakia lost 3 million citizens and a defensible frontier. Six months later, Hitler occupied the Czech areas as well, and Slovakia became a satellite state of Nazi Germany. Under the force of Nazi aggression, the country that Masaryk had worked so hard to build no longer existed.

The 85-year-old father of the Czechoslovak republic, Tomáš Masaryk, resigns from office on December 14, 1935. Beneš, Masaryk's successor as president of Czechoslovakia, took office just as Hitler embarked on his quest for world domination.

Then came World War II, and Hitler's Germany was destroyed in its turn. Czechoslovakia was restored, but it was no longer the country of Masaryk's dreams: The prediction of the doubters during World War I had come true. Though liberated from Nazi Germany, Czechoslovakia was now part of the sphere of influence of Soviet Russia. In February 1948 the Communist party of Czechoslovakia seized power. Masaryk's son Jan, serving as foreign minister at the time, fell to his death from a window of the foreign ministry building. Though the official explanation called it a suicide, the death of Jan Masaryk is to this day an unsolved mystery. Beneš, who had returned as president after the war, died in October 1948 and was replaced by the Communist leader Klement Gottwald. Czechoslovakia has been a Communist country ever since.

Apart from a brief period of ferment that was ended by Soviet intervention in 1968, Communist rule in Czechoslovakia has been repressive ever since the takeover in 1948. Instead of acting as a beacon of progress to the world, as Masaryk had hoped, the Czechs have lost ground among the economically and culturally advanced nations. The Communists reject Masaryk's idea of linking the fate of Czechoslovakia with that of all humanity.

Czech citizens pay tribute to Masaryk on the occasion of his death, September 14, 1937. Though foreign powers — the Nazis in the 1930s and later the Soviets — have undone much of Masaryk's achievement, the memory of the greatest Czech statesman remains today an inspiration for Czechs and for all peoples subject to foreign domination.

Instead, they proclaim that their country is one of a small and tightly knit group of nations, in which it has the modest rank of a follower, not a leader. An endlessly repeated Communist slogan praises "the firm unity of the Socialist countries, headed by the Soviet Union." For the time being, at least, Czechoslovakia has given up Masaryk's dream of being a small country with a great destiny in a world of equal nations.

All the same, Masaryk's achievement has lasting significance. The country he built may not so far have fulfilled his hopes, but the present and the likely future of the Czechs and Slovaks are better than their past. For both nations, being part of an internationally recognized independent country, even one that bows to the Soviet Union, helps ensure that their traditions, languages, and cultural achievements will never be extinguished. In a world of superpower politics, Masaryk's insistence on the value of small nations to the human race, and their equality with big nations, may seem unrealisitic. Yet it is far nobler to strive toward this ideal, as Masaryk did, than to worship naked force.

Prague Spring. Czech and Slovak national pride, widespread discontent, and a spirit of hope combined to spark a reform movement in Czechoslovakia in 1968. Eventually the Soviets sent in tanks to put a stop to the movement.

Masaryk was certainly far from being the faultless hero that his devoted followers worshiped. On the contrary, he was a living example of the truth that the most splendid qualities, when carried to extremes, become defects. His disciples and friends extolled his independence of character, his fearless honesty, his courage and persistence, and strength of will. Others, not necessarily his enemies, shook their head over his haughty intolerance, his indifference to the views and feelings of others, his obstinacy and rashness, and fanatical obsessiveness. Throughout his life, he was at his best in crises, scandals, and extreme situations, and when the hour of war and revolution struck, he rose to the moment and achieved greatness. When destiny summoned him, both his virtues and his faults combined to enable him to do great deeds.

During his long life, Tomáš Masaryk—professor of philosophy, writer, political activist, diplomat, liberator, and world leader—proved that unwavering determination can give birth to a nation. Since Masaryk's death, decades of subjugation have not broken the spirit of the Czech people, who continue to derive strength from his example.

Further Reading

Beneš, Edvard. *Masaryk's Path and Legacy.* New York: Arno, 1971.

Čapek, Karel. *President Masaryk Tells His Story.* New York: Putnam, 1935.

Hajek, Hanus J. *T. G. Masaryk Revisited.* New York: Columbia University Press, 1983.

Kerner, Robert J., ed. *Czechoslovakia.* Berkeley: University of California Press, 1949.

Korbel, Joseph. *Twentieth-Century Czechoslovakia: The Meaning of Its History.* New York: Columbia University Press, 1977.

Kovtun, George J. *The Czechoslovak Declaration of Independence: A History of the Document.* Washington, DC: Library of Congress, 1985.

Mamatey, Victor S., and Radomir Luza. *A History of the Czechoslovak Republic 1918–1948.* Princeton: Princeton University Press, 1973.

Masaryk, Tomáš G. *The Meaning of Czech History.* Chapel Hill: University of North Carolina Press, 1974.

Saxon-Ford, Stephanie. *The Czech Americans.* New York: Chelsea House, 1989.

Selver, Paul. *Masaryk: A Biography.* Westport, CT: Greenwood Press, 1975.

Stolarik, M. Mark. *The Slovak Americans.* New York: Chelsea House, 1988.

Szporluk, Roman. *The Political Thought of Tomas G. Masaryk.* New York: Columbia University Press, 1981.

Thomson, S. Harrison. *Czechoslovakia in European History.* Princeton: Princeton University Press, 1953.

Wallace, William V. *Czechoslovakia.* Boulder, CO: Westview Press, 1976.

Chronology

March 7, 1850	Born Tomáš Masaryk in Hodonín, Moravia, a province of what was then Austria-Hungary
1865–79	Studies in Brno, Moravia, and Vienna
March 15, 1878	Marries Charlotte Garrigue in Brooklyn, New York; adopts name of Tomáš Garrigue Masaryk
Aug. 13, 1882	Receives appointment to professor of philosophy at University of Prague
1886–87	Helps prove that manuscripts venerated as containing ancient Czech poetry are forged
1891–93	Wins election to the Vienna parliament; spends summer of 1902 in the United States; resigns from paraliament and returns to academic life
1899–1900	Defends Leopold Hilsner, a Jew accused of murder
March 31, 1900	Named leader of the newly founded Realist party
May 1907	Reelected to the Vienna parliament
1910–11	Implicates Minister of Foreign Affairs Baron Alois von Aehrenthal in a forgery and consipiracy scandal
July 1914	World War I begins
Dec. 18, 1914	Masaryk goes into exile
Sept. 24, 1915	Accepts appointment as professor of Slavic studies at King's College, University of London
March 14, 1917	Outbreak of the February Revolution in Russia
July–Oct. 1917	Masaryk recruits former prisoners of war to form the 40,000-man Czechoslovak Legion
Nov. 7, 1917	Outbreak of the October Revolution in Russia
May 14, 1918	Czechoslovak Legion clashes with Bolsheviks and seizes control of the Trans-Siberian Railroad
July 13, 1918	Czechoslovak National Committee formed in Prague
Oct. 28, 1918	Proclamation of Czechoslovak independence in Prague
Nov. 14, 1918	Masaryk elected president of Czechoslovakia by the Provisional National Assembly
1919–20	Paris Peace Conference awards Slovakia, Bohemia, Moravia, and Silesia to Czechoslovakia
Oct. 1921	Formation of the Little Entente between Czechoslovakia, Yugoslavia, and Romania
Jan. 25, 1924	Treaty of alliance between Czechoslovakia and France
Dec. 14, 1935	Masaryk resigns as president of Czechoslovakia and is succeeded by Edvard Beneš
Sept. 14, 1937	Masaryk dies at Lany, near Prague

Index

Gavin Lewis teaches history at John Jay College in New York City. He received his B.A. from Oxford University, England, and his Ph.D. from Princeton University. The author of numerous works on the political and social history of central Europe, he is currently at work on a series of historical case studies, ranging from ancient Mesopotamia to the present day, for college students.

Arthur M. Schlesinger, jr., taught history at Harvard for many years and is currently Albert Schweitzer Professor of the Humanities at City University of New York. He is the author of numerous highly praised works in American history and has twice been awarded the Pulitzer Prize. He served in the White House as special assistant to Presidents Kennedy and Johnson.

PICTURE CREDITS

The Balch Institute: p. 68; The Bettmann Archive: pp. 30, 31, 32, 41, 42, 47, 55, 56, 62, 65, 74, 75, 94, 103; Culver Pictures: pp. 23, 27, 38, 39, 40, 66, 67, 79, 83; Koudelka/Magnum Photos: p. 106; The Library of Congress: pp. 21, 22, 81; The New York Public Library, Slavonic Division: pp. 2, 14, 20, 25, 26, 28, 34, 45, 52, 73, 91, 100, 107; Donna Sinisgalli: p. 92; University of California at Berkeley Library: pp. 18, 24, 36, 50, 80, 84; University of Chicago Library, Special Collections: p. 53; UPI/Bettmann Newsphotos: pp. 12, 16–17, 54, 60, 64, 76, 78, 83, 86, 87, 90, 97, 101, 102, 104, 105